RUN THE RACE

RUN THE RACE

A FATHER'S LEGACY OF LIFE LESSONS

Susan Z. Dawes

iUniverse, Inc.
New York Lincoln Shanghai

Run the Race
A Father's Legacy of Life Lessons

Copyright © 2007 by Susan Z. Dawes

iUniverse books may be ordered through booksellers or by contacting:

iUniverse
2021 Pine Lake Road, Suite 100
Lincoln, NE 68512
www.iuniverse.com
1-800-Authors (1-800-288-4677)

ISBN: 978-0-595-42942-4 (pbk)
ISBN: 978-0-595-87284-8 (ebk)

Printed in the United States of America

In loving memory of my father, Floyd Henry Seibert,
who still inspires me every day to keep running.

It is a wise father that knows his own child.
William Shakespeare

Contents

Acknowledgments

As with any book, there are many people to thank.

First, I give glory to God for always taking care of me.

My mom for her sustaining love, prayers, and for showing me what faith is all about.

To my daughters—Sara, Anna, and Maria, for their support and patience during this entire process. You are my greatest blessings.

To my brothers, Denny and Randy, and sister, Sheila, for creating many fun childhood memories and confirming information. Family is forever.

Terri Clamons, my friend and mentor. I'm grateful for all the brunches where we discussed this project.

Ann Ingalls, for her friendship and invaluable advice. I'm so thankful we met that day at the mailbox.

Susan Ashby, my beach buddy, for mentioning I should write a book about growing up with a great dad.

Carol Newman, a writing teacher who motivated me to publish this manuscript.

Barb Brown Trier, a great runner who responded to many emails.

My friends in Corolla, North Carolina, who provided a perfect escape to write.

Kirsten Mc Bride, for her last-minute editing.

The staff at iUniverse, especially Rachele Walter.

All those I mentioned who have impacted my life.

And finally, to everyone who encouraged me through this journey of writing, thank you.

Introduction: Meet My Coach

This book came about during my routine morning run one day. It was toward the end of the course, as I was heading up the hill. I started to slow down and thought about quitting, until my devoted running buddy, Daisy, the family English setter, glanced back over her shoulder with that inquisitive expression, *Are you quitting now? We are almost finished.* Not wanting to disappoint her or myself, I took off sprinting with what energy I had left. That's when the ideas ignited in my mind. The moment I entered the house, I put a pen to paper. It was January 14, 2004.

The real inspiration, though, for this book is my dad. It began one night in 1972, when he invited me, a seventh grader, to attend a high school girls' track meet so I could watch long-distance runners. I knew instantly these races were meant for me.

The foundation for this book is built upon one significant comment Dad made after I was defeated in a race and wanted to quit. He said, "There will always be another race to run." I strongly sensed from the way he said it that this wasn't just about the races on the track or cross-country runs. It was much larger than that. It was about running the races of life.

Dad became my sideline coach during track as well as throughout many of my life experiences. He not only knew how to cultivate my athletic skills, but he also taught me about living—one race at a time. And he accomplished this through his guidance and love.

He was compassionate, kind, patient, and humble. He could be trusted and had integrity, always willing to lend a helping hand to his family or those in need. I suppose you could say he lived an ordinary life, but was an extraordinary father. He knew his purpose in life and took it seriously.

Born to Charles and Pearl Seibert, he grew up on a farm with his parents and two older brothers, Marion and LaVere, in Minburn, Iowa. On several occasions, I heard Dad describe his childhood. *We did not have very much, but we were loved.*

My dad had a strong interest in sports early on in life. Throughout his childhood, and particularly during his high-school years, his time was spent either on the basketball court shooting hoops or on the field pitching a fastball for the baseball team. And from his friends' accounts, Floyd was quite a treat to watch as he played.

Baseball became his real passion after he graduated from high school. The New York Yankees scouted him and drafted him into their farm club. This sent him on the road playing games in the southeastern quadrant of the United States, a place he had only known about from geography class.

Dad delighted in telling the story about seeing the Atlantic Ocean for the first time. He was so excited he ran into the water, where he was instantly pulled down by the undercurrent. He thought he was a goner because no one had ever taught him how to swim. Fortunately, he managed to tumble back to shore safely.

My dad did not finish his dream of playing baseball in the big leagues. According to my mom, his mother made a visit to the Georgia coast where he was living. She disapproved of the conditions in the rundown motels and boarding houses that the players stayed in back then. However, the real determining factor was that his father needed help on the farm, so Dad, being a loyal son, returned home to help farm but not for long.

He soon grew restless with the farming routine and sought other opportunities. Iowa Power and Light—considered a solid company—is where he would be employed for the next thirty-eight years. He was hired as a line man but was promoted to a service man after a few years. Dad enjoyed his work and was proud to work for the company, but he did not love his work more than his family. Work very rarely interfered with his personal life.

My dad's life was centered on his dedication to his family. After my parents married in 1950, they were blessed with four children. Floyd Dennis (Denny) was born November 19, 1954. Randy followed on September 21, 1957. I was next, arriving on January 25, 1959. Our baby sister, Sheila, was born on May 29, 1961.

Dad was extremely proud of his children, and it always showed, especially as he taught us the ins and outs of many athletic activities. He taught us how to ride our bikes, shoot baskets, and pitch baseballs or softballs. But the night Dad introduced me to long-distance running was the moment that changed my life. It became a sport I loved. And in life, it became a saving grace.

This story is about more than running races around a track. It is about a strong bond between a father and daughter. It is about a father's sustaining presence throughout many triumphant times and trying trials of life. It is about a loving father who taught his daughter about living and not giving up during life's many races.

First Race:
Finding a Race

*The answer to the big questions in running is the same as the
answer to the big questions in life;
do the best with what you've got.*

George Sheehan, MD, marathon runner and author

Life presents many races to run. A few may take place on a
track. The majority will be run off the track. Results will vary.
In some you may be victorious, in some you will struggle. In
others you will never win, no matter how hard you try.

Finding a race I could run well for the upcoming junior-
high track season was like that for me. It was the summer of
1971, and I had just finished sixth grade. I was already excited
in anticipation of entering junior high school. I knew that
graduating to the next level would open up more opportunities for participating in organized sports. And I had set my
sights on becoming a track star. I wanted to be good at something. Every child does.

I knew that to be good, practice was essential. I had learned this from watching my brothers, Denny and Randy, whom I considered great all-around athletes. Both ran track and did it well.

I decided to focus at first on the low hurdles. I turned to Dad for help with this new mission on my mind. Dad was more than willing to help and drove me many times to the track so I could practice. He coached me from the sidelines on proper form. However, one evening he decided instead to watch the high-school girls' softball game adjacent to the track. I was fine with this because I was feeling very confident in what I was doing.

I set up the hurdles in order on the track and started running and jumping over them. I had watched and studied many good hurdlers over the years. Denny, my oldest brother, was one of them. He was known all over the state of Iowa for his success in the high hurdles. I loved watching him skim over the tops of those hurdles. He attacked them with such grace that he made it look easy. That evening, it was on my mind to emulate his "skimming" style. I was just getting the hang of it when the dreaded event happened.

I hit the top of a hurdle with my right leg and went tumbling onto the cinder track, every body part, except my face, hitting the rough, dark surface. For a few minutes, I lay on the track in agony until I rolled over and slowly pulled myself into a sitting position to survey the damage. I was a mess. Blood oozed from the palms of my hands and from my arms, elbows, knees, and shins. My worst bicycle wrecks paled in comparison to this, which would go down as the worst wipeout of my life. I slowly stood up, and with tears streaming down my cheeks, pathetically limped off to find Dad.

I spotted him standing behind the softball backstop chatting to a friend. I sensed they were involved in a deep discussion over the game. When I appeared, all talking stopped abruptly, and a ghastly look appeared on Dad's face.

"Sue, what happened to you?"

"I wiped out on the hurdles," I tearfully explained.

Without hesitation, Dad scooped me up in his arms.

"You need to see Dr. Hanlon to make sure you're OK."

And within minutes we were headed back to our house to phone Dr. Hanlon.

Dr. Hanlon was the town physician, and everyone knew they could call him day or night. This was an evening call; he met us promptly at his office to inspect the damage. He took one look at me and reiterated what my dad had asked: "What happened to you?" After I explained my embarrassing wipeout on the hurdles, he immediately started gently but firmly digging out the cinders from my wounds. Dad stood beside the examining table with his hand on my shoulder and reassured me that everything would be OK. Dr. Hanlon then cleaned the wounds after extracting most of the cinders except for those still in my left knee. "That scar will be with you forever," he said.

After that fall you might assume I would have given up hope of being a hurdler. But, oh no, I was even more determined to run those hurdles. When the junior-high track season started the following spring, there I was again, practicing and trying my darnedest to improve my form and time.

Coach Gunderson was an exceptional coach. He let everyone participate in something. I tried out for the shuttle-hurdle relay. I earned a spot—but on the "B" team. I was disappointed but continued to practice.

Then one spring evening in 1972, a window of hope opened up to me. Dad invited me to watch a girls' high-school track meet being held in my hometown of Adel, Iowa. It was a bone-chilling evening. I stood shivering beside my dad under a towering maple tree and watched intently.

That night, Dad was anxious for me to observe both the half-mile run and the mile relay. His comment still echoes today: "Sue, maybe you would like to run long distances some day like those girls."

Dad had an instinct for cultivating children's athletic abilities. I'm sure that evolved from his natural athletic talents, along with his playing experience with the New York Yankees' farm club. And over the years, he was recognized for being a winning coach for my brothers' little league baseball teams—the Dallas County Yankees.

On this evening, he pointed out the differences in short- versus long-distance racing. It was obvious the shorter races required speed. He stressed that the longer distances required endurance.

It didn't take much convincing on Dad's part to get me to focus on the quarter-mile run. I was instantly attracted to the longer distances, because it was evident from my childhood experiences that I was not considered a high-speed runner.

Every child growing up in a small town looks forward to the annual races with great anticipation. I was no exception. There was one special event that took place on the Saturday before Easter—the Easter-egg hunt at Nile Kinnick Park in Adel.

I can still remember riding to the park with my parents, two older brothers, and younger sister for this big event. As soon as we arrived and Dad parked the car, I was eagerly opening the door to get a good view of the wide-open field which glistened with cellophane-wrapped Easter eggs.

Nile Kinnick Park was the perfect setting for the excited kids who arrived with their parents. The enthusiasm echoed loudly in the air before this race. Each child carried decorated baskets or brown paper grocery bags. Some even wore their Easter bonnets. In the center of the park was the field where the race would take place. To the left was the public swimming pool and red playground equipment with several picnic tables. The softball field was situated on the right, adjacent to a football field that was encircled by a track. A track that—little did I know at the time—held a future for me.

The central area of the park was always divided by age group. I had been attending these hunts since the age of two. My memories start from the age of six.

It was the same strategic plan every year for the event. Some eggs were plain; others had a white tag attached to their cellophane wrapper. The objective: go for the white tag attached to the cellophane-wrapped, pastel marshmallow egg.

Inevitably, the fastest runners would be the victors. The race only lasted a minute or so, and it was amazing how quickly those eggs disappeared. I ran as fast as my little legs could carry me to grab those eggs and toss them in my basket, but no matter how hard I tried, I was never fortunate enough to get many with white tags. Most of my eggs were considered the "leftovers"—the ones that had been stepped on or the plain ones with no tags.

The eggs with white tags were valuable, because they were traded for money. After each race, we piled back into the car, and Dad chauffeured us to the stores on the town square. There I would present my few tags to the owner or sales clerk and redeem them for the lucrative winnings. The price range was five cents to a dollar. The "golden egg," valued at a dollar, was what every child hoped for; however, those were few and far between. I never scored a golden egg, but my brothers did. Their baskets overflowed with tagged eggs. Often, they shared some of those coveted eggs with me.

The other significant running event for kids was the annual track-and-field day. The elementary school my two brothers, sister, and I attended hosted this at the end of each school year. It was a day filled with races and relays—another event which required speed to do well.

It was the same scenario as the Easter-egg hunt. The fastest kids made out like bandits on track-and-field day. Everyone received at least one ribbon for participation. The teachers made sure of that. But on an individual basis, I never placed first or even second.

And like always, my siblings excelled on this day. They viewed it as an exciting day and couldn't wait to run home with blue and red ribbons clutched in their hands for "show and tell" at the dinner table that evening. I never had much to say or to show after this big day. I just listened and secretly wished I had speed like them.

However, on this spring night in 1972, standing alongside Dad, something different took place. Within me there was a feeling of hope and excitement about running.

When the track meet ended, I told Dad I was going to run a lap around the track. As I ran, he watched with concentration from the sidelines and yelled words of encouragement. As I rounded the last corner toward the finish line, he waved and told me to keep running.

Dad caught up with me at the finish line.

He said, "Sue, you looked good out there running."

He also commented that I had the right stride and pace for running longer distances. Dad always had a way of pointing out the positive.

It was an exciting ride home that night. As he drove, I sat in the passenger's seat bursting with happiness. I felt as though I had finally found something I could do well. Maybe I could even win a few races.

I told Dad that night that I wanted to be a long-distance runner.

He replied with a smile, "Good. I hear they are adding the quarter-mile run next year for junior-high track. Maybe that will be your race."

As I reflect on this first race, I have come to a conclusion. Dad realized that I was never going to be a sprinter or hurdler but would find long-distance running appealing. He never verbally said that. He was too kind and diplomatic to tell me I didn't have the speed of my two older brothers and younger sister.

Thankfully, Dad was extremely intuitive and wise. He redirected my attention to running the longer distances. He applied this same wisdom when it came to teaching me about running many other races in life.

One lap around the track that spring evening in 1972, and I was hooked on something that would help me through the journey of life more than I could have ever imagined.

Second Race:
Simple Advice

Winning is not everything, but the effort to win is.

Zig Ziglar

The opportunity to prove myself occurred in spring of 1973. The Adel Junior High Tigerette track squad added the quarter mile that year. I claimed it as my race.

Looking back, I may have been the only person who dared to sign up to run this race. To most girls, it appeared intimidating and exhausting. To me, it was a challenge and one that I was more than willing to try. I made up my mind that I could do this and do it well.

It was evident during pre-season that the coach was training me for the long-distance, which was just fine with me. I trained hard and gave it my best. A week before the first track meet, Coach Gunderson told me I would represent our squad in the quarter-mile run as the number-one runner for my team.

The night before the big track meet, I was a bundle of nerves. Dad tried to ease my fears by going over with me what I needed to do to get through the race. Not win the race—just finish the race.

He shared with me his nervousness before baseball games.

"I used to get nervous before I pitched."

"What did you do?" I asked.

"I would take a deep breath, say a short prayer, tell myself I could do this, and then go and pitch the game as best I could. You can do that, too. Just go out and run the race."

Simple advice, but it worked. It not only worked for this particular race, but for many races yet to come, on, as well as off, the track.

The anticipated day arrived. We traveled to Norwalk, Iowa, for the junior-high track meet. My parents were both present. Mom sat in the bleachers and chatted with the other parents. Dad stood behind the fence a few feet from the starting line. He was still in his work clothes and wore his Iowa Power and Light hat. This was a perfect strategic spot for him to watch me begin the race. He had his usual words of encouragement that day. He shouted, "Sue, pace yourself. You can do this!" Then he gave a quick wave above his head and smiled.

So I nodded and remembered his advice from the night before. I took a deep breath, prayed, told myself I could run this quarter mile, and concentrated on the sound of the starting gun. Once the gun fired, I was off and running.

There is always one runner who takes off sprinting as though she were running the hundred-yard dash. My coach had already warned me about this type of runner. What he advised was that initially, you come out sprinting to grab the lead, and then slow down and set the pace. So I came out sprinting and set the pace, momentarily forgetting about that one girl sprinting ahead like a fool who would, in no time, run out of speed. I grabbed the lead, but could feel the presence of another runner behind me, right on my heels. I still had the lead as I rounded the last corner of the track to head toward the finish line. Then I caught a glimpse of Dad standing behind the fence along the track yelling, "Sue, you have to kick it, she's coming around you!"

I dug my cleats in deeper and gave it the best sprint I had left down the home stretch toward the finish line. We were neck and neck for a few steps but she was faster and out-sprinted me to cross the finish line a good stride ahead of me. I finished second. The only consolation for winning second was that it was the first time the race had ever been run for my school, so it went down as a record for Adel Junior High.

Dad hastily approached the finish line with a radiant smile. By his glowing face you would have thought I'd placed first.

"Good job, Sue. You looked great out there running that lap!"

"But I got second; she beat me at the finish line," I said.

His response to my dissatisfaction was, "Sue, you did great running your first quarter-mile. You did your best. It's not always about being first; it's that you finished and didn't give up." Then he invited me to the concession stand for a treat. He rewarded me with a Mountain Dew and a Snickers bar. This became our ritual at future track meets.

The quarter-mile proved to be my race. I finally found an event I was proud to participate in. Overall, this track season proved to be a successful one for me. I worked on getting my time down and even placed first in the conference meet. Dad was always present at every track meet. I always knew where to look for him. If it was a home meet, he would stand under the towering sunset maple tree near the starting line at the first turn on the track. Then he would hustle down to the last turn on the track as I headed toward the finish line. I counted on Dad to coach me from the sidelines. And he never let me down.

Running became a big part of my life. I finally found a sport that I absolutely loved. I will always be grateful to my dad for cultivating my interest in running. He also instilled in me the belief that it was not about winning every race, but doing your best and never giving up.

It was always the same scenario. He stood along the track cheering me on until I crossed the finish line. After each race, with a "proud father" smile on his face, he would rush over to find me, no matter what place I'd won. He was the greatest sideline coach ever. He was the greatest dad, too.

Third Race: Longer Distances

Whatever you are, be a good one.

Abraham Lincoln

Cross-country season started in fall of 1973, my freshman year. Adel was known around the state of Iowa for having a competitive cross-country team. And this season, it so happened we had an individual predicted to win the state meet. Barb Brown was her name. She was not only a great runner, but a great mentor for me.

Pre-season went well. My practice times impressed Coach Gunderson so much that he placed me as the second runner on the team roster. I was healthy, well-conditioned, and ready to run longer distances than the quarter-mile.

Cross-country running is not for everyone. In fact, the name "cross country" means just what it says: you run long distances on country roads.

Our school practices consisted of at least a five-mile warm-up. Typically, our coach would drop us off somewhere in the country and tell us to run back to the track in town. Once back at the track, we would run more distance races along with some sprint work.

That fall season, my hometown of Adel, as always, was alive with vibrant foliage. Adel is situated twenty miles west of Des Moines, the state capital. This small town, with a population of barely three thousand, is located in a valley with the Raccoon River winding around the outskirts. The landscape is filled with rolling green hills and a variety of big trees. Farmland surrounds the town for miles.

As an avid nature lover from childhood, cross-country running was extremely enjoyable to me. Barb had taught me to look ahead for a target to run toward to make the time pass. I usually picked a sign, big tree, or barn. Once I reached that marker, I would focus on something else. It did keep my mind preoccupied while running those miles.

Overall, my coach, my parents, and I were pleased with the way my freshman season was progressing. My first cross-country meet was at Hoover High School in Des Moines. Coach Gunderson let me run for the junior varsity team. I won first place with a time of 9:56 for a mile and a half, receiving my first trophy ever. I was so proud of that trophy.

When it came to the varsity meets, Barb Brown always placed first. I ran as the second runner for my team and would finish either second or somewhere in the top twenty, which was OK with me. I realized I was never going to beat Barb. Instead, I found enjoyment in the competition and the experience of running with some of the best high-school athletes in the state. At that time in athletics, there were no class divisions based on the size of the high-school population. This made it very competitive, to say the least.

The state championship was always held at the end of the season on a Saturday in late October. This big event was held in Adel at Hillcrest Country Club, which was to our advantage, for we were allowed to take practice runs on the course. Coach Gunderson had high hopes for our team and me. He was confident Barb would place first and I would be in the top thirty. As predicted, Barb Brown secured the first-place spot with ease. I was quite a ways back from her, coming in second for our team, but in the seventy-first spot overall out of the 154 participants who ran that day. As a team, we placed ninth.

It was obvious this was not a good race day for me. I was disgusted I had let the team down with my poor performance. I blamed it on having to run in a sleeveless top and brief shorts in the unusually cold weather that morning. The large number of runners psyched me out too.

As expected, Dad was waiting for me at the finish line after the race. He just hugged me and tried to find the positive in my disappointing performance. He reassured me that for my first state race, and only being a freshman, I had done a good job. Most importantly, I finished the race.

Track season followed in the spring of my freshman year. By now, I was considered a long-distance runner. Coach Niemeyer was the high-school girls' track coach. He was well known all over the state of Iowa for being an extremely competitive and winning coach. He also yelled a lot, which intensified my nervousness. However, he recognized my talent for long distance and trained me for the 880 run and mile run.

Barb Brown was again the number-one 880 and mile runner for our team, while I secured the second-place spot. I didn't mind being second fiddle behind Barb. In fact, I became accustomed to getting second, until one race in May of 1974.

That conference meet took place in Norwalk, Iowa. This was the same track where I had run my first competitive race as an eighth grader and lost on the home stretch. However, Coach Niemeyer was confident I would place second behind Barb Brown in the half-mile run.

Everything appeared to be perfect that evening, aside from one major thing. Dad was nowhere in sight. He was always at every race and had assured me that morning before he left for work that he would be there. The runners had not lined up on the track yet, so I took the opportunity to size up the competition.

I had run against everyone in past meets with the exception of one girl. I recognized her by her long, black-braided ponytail. Her name was Josie, and she was from Dallas Center. But she was a sprinter, so I discounted her ability to run the 880.

I told myself that if I ran this race strategically, I would place second, just like Coach Niemeyer predicted. But where was my dad? He was my sideline coach. He was the one I listened to when I ran my races. I needed him there for support. I also needed him to yell my lap time, and more importantly, to warn me of encroaching runners.

As I stepped onto the track and approached my lane assignment, I heard the distinct roar in the distance and smiled. The roar came from Dad's diesel work truck. As I looked up on the hill, I could see the Iowa Power and Light truck pulling into the parking lot. He tooted the horn and waved out the driver's window as if to say, *I made it, Sue. Now run the race.*

I smiled and waved back confidently. Now I was ready to run.

The race began, and I sprinted out and placed myself as the second runner behind Barb Brown. Barb set the pace, and I followed. In my mind, being second to her was like being first. No one came close to beating Barb.

When we rounded the corner to finish the first lap, Dad was standing in his usual place cheering for me and Barb. He yelled for me to keep up the good pace.

I felt good running the next lap, which was the last lap of the 880 run. The adrenaline was pumping full force, and I knew I would have some extra energy left over to kick it at the end of this lap. At this point, Barb started to pull away for first place.

As I rounded the last corner to head down the final stretch, I caught a glimpse of my dad, who had placed himself at his usual spot at the end of the track. He was jumping up and down, hollering. "Kick it harder! Sue, you have one coming up on you. Give it all you've got."

It was evident from the uproar coming out of the bleachers and sidelines that she was too close for comfort and must be on my heels.

To this day, I still relive the final moments of that race. I can feel myself reaching down deep for every last ounce of energy in my body. I thought for sure I had second place secured, but three feet from the finish line, the sprinter from Dallas Center—who had never run an 880—ran past me and crossed the finish line by one stride. She beat me.

Words cannot describe how I felt that evening. I was totally stunned.

As I came to a halt, I bent over to catch my breath. I felt sick to my stomach—a combination of overexertion and the taste of defeat.

As soon as I regained my composure, I walked over and congratulated the girl who had come from nowhere and beat me.

That's another thing Dad taught me: *Never be a sore loser.*

Within minutes, Dad was standing by my side. He immediately gave me one of his side hugs and told me what a great race I had run.

I remember looking up at him. "But she beat me at the finish line. I knew I couldn't beat Barb, but I was supposed to come in second. She wasn't even a long-distance runner."

"You gave it your best. You didn't give up, and you finished the race. Third place is still good." Then he invited me to the concession stand for my Mountain Dew and Snickers bar, which helped ease the pain of defeat a little bit.

Even though I was running in second place most of the time, I still felt I was a good runner. Running these races on the track was teaching me some important lessons that could be applied to life. I learned things do not always go your way even when you think you had it all planned out. Always accept defeat graciously although you may not think it is fair. And most importantly—do your best and finish the race.

Fourth Race:
Pacing Myself

A runner's creed: I will win; if I cannot win, I shall be second; if I cannot be second, I shall be third; if I cannot place at all, I shall do my best.

Ken Doherty, famous running coach and trainer

The fall of 1974 brought another cross-country season. I was a sophomore, and Coach Gunderson had big dreams for me. Barb Brown, the star runner of the state and my mentor, had graduated in May. Expectations were high for me to be the number-one runner for the team and to place well in the state track meet.

However, this season would prove to be a very frustrating one, in the form of a freshman by the name of Sue McIlrath. She had broken my junior-high record in the quarter-mile with ease. She was giving me a run for my money in pre-season training. By the time the official season started, she and I were battling for the number-one spot on the team. And on top of all that, her name was Sue, too.

That's the way the season unfolded. Sometimes I would win. Other times she placed first—until the Urbandale Invitational. It was the last scheduled meet before Districts. For some reason, I had concluded she would probably beat me on this course. I had even voiced that prediction to Dad at the breakfast table that morning.

"I'll probably get beat by McIlrath today," I said.

"You can't think that way before a race. You have to think positive and tell yourself you will have a good run. You ran on that course last year. You know the layout, which should help you. You know I'll be there."

Dad was definitely there. He showed up early and gave me a pep talk.

"Remember to pace yourself and save some for the end because of the hill. You can do this, Sue. Just go out and run the race the best you can."

It was a gorgeous Indian-summer day. The meet was being held at the Urbandale Golf and Country Club. This course was tough because of the "killer hill" toward the end of the race. I ran this course as a freshman and the memory still lingered.

I went through the routine ritual of stretching and psyching myself up with my standard, motivational pep talk.

You can do this.
Pace yourself.
Attack the hills.
Keep your arms low.

Breathe.

The announcer took the microphone.

"Runners, please line up. Get set." The gun was fired.

And we were all off to the races.

I sprinted toward the front and stayed close to Sue McIlrath and Kathy Pitcock from Earlham. The three of us ran together over a mile.

Kathy took the lead and started to pull away. I could see that McIlrath was struggling with her breathing and pacing. At that point, I was running with ease and decided to pass McIlrath as we headed up the dreaded hill.

To my surprise, there stood Dad alone, halfway up the hill. He had never positioned himself on the course during cross-country meets. He always waited for me at the finish line. However, this day was different. Today, he must have sensed I needed him standing right there to coach me up that hill.

The huge hill started to take its toll on me. My breathing became labored, and I felt my body tightening. I wanted desperately to walk. As I approached where Dad was standing, I panted, "I can't do this." He got right next to me and jogged along with me for a few steps.

"Come on, Sue, lean into the hill, lower your arms, and breathe. When you get to the top of the hill, you have less than a 440 to run. You can do this. Don't give up now. Go after Kathy."

Those were the exact words I needed to hear. They energized my mind and body. I wanted to win this race. I had beaten Kathy before, so I started to tell myself I could do this.

And I knew that in a few minutes, win or lose, the race would be over.

I did exactly as my dad had said. When I reached the top of the hill, I dug my cleats in deep and pushed the pace up a notch. But I couldn't catch Kathy. She had gotten too much of a lead on me. I crossed the finish line in second place, a place that by now was very familiar to me. Dad appeared shortly after to give me a big hug and words of praise for my performance. I started complaining about getting second again and that I should have run smarter, but he didn't care that I placed second. He reiterated something I already knew, *it was about not giving up on that huge hill to finish the race.*

The cross-country season came to a close with the state meet being held at Hillcrest Country Club, again in Adel, a course I had run many times by now. It was a sunny but very chilly Saturday morning. Our team was predicted to do well, and I was again to finish in the top thirty. However, for me this race turned out to be a disaster.

There were 152 runners qualified to run. Obviously, lining up that many girls took some organization. But once that was accomplished, we were all raring to run. The announcer made his usual proclamation and then fired the starting gun.

Within seconds of starting, a runner behind me spiked my ankle with her metal cleat, catching the back of my shoe. A runner's nightmare ensued. My shoe came flying off. I made a split decision to run the race without the shoe, rather than quit.

I was doomed from the start, but I still ran the race with one shoe and a bloody ankle. Mentally and physically, I was already defeated. I tried running on grass as much as possible, but there were a few trails with rocks, which pierced the bottom of my foot. I was distressed, but I finished the race and placed ninety-ninth. Dad was anxiously waiting for me at the finish line. He knew something had gone wrong because of my placement. I burst into tears the minute I crossed the finish line and told him what had happened. He wrapped his arm around me and said, "Most people would have quit, and you didn't. I'm very proud of you for that." And then with his arm still around me, we went and looked for my shoe.

That was how I concluded my last cross-country race in high school. The school board passed a new ruling for the following season. Athletes could only participate in one fall sport. At that point, I was playing fall softball and running cross-country. To play softball you needed to participate in both the summer and fall seasons, so I reluctantly gave up cross-country running but looked forward to running track in the spring.

A week before spring track season started, I tried out to be a cheerleader for the wrestling team. My brother Randy was a varsity wrestler, so I already had a vested interest in the team. As I was ending my tryout routine, I decided to impress everyone by ending in the splits. When I landed, something popped in my left leg. I slowly stood up in pain and limped over to the bleacher, only steps away. Later that day, Dr. Hanlon diagnosed it as a pulled hamstring. Not good news to announce to Coach Niemeyer, the track coach.

I secured a place on the cheerleading squad, but in doing so jeopardized my position on the track team. At every practice and every meet, my injured leg had to be prepped. The trainer would slap a big glob of red pain-relieving cream on the left hamstring, followed with a gauze patch and an Ace bandage. It was not unusual for the wrap to come undone while I ran, which embarrassed me. It looked like I had a flag flying from my leg.

Even with my injury, I was still improving my time, but I was back in the second-place position, running behind freshman Sue McIlrath. I didn't like being beaten by a freshman, but I had accepted it. I ran the 880 and the mile run at every meet. The mile event was my favorite, and I qualified for State that year with a time of 5:47.

During track season of my junior year after a mile run, I told Dad I wanted to quit. It was my pride. I was getting tired of running second behind McIlrath, an underclassman. Dad was very straightforward with me that evening. He said, "I'm not going to let you quit, Sue. You did your best out there tonight." And then he said something I will never forget: "There will always be another race to run." It was the way he said it and the look in his trusting blue eyes that made me think he wasn't just talking about the races on the track. It was as if he were talking about races in the future, the races in life we have to run. After that night, I never brought up quitting track again.

The last track meet of my senior year was held in Urbandale, Iowa, at the high school. It was the last meet I would ever run as an Adel Tigerette. Coach Niemeyer pulled me aside and said I would be running the first anchor of the mile relay, the 880 run, and the mile run. Then he said, "You will be running as our number-one runner tonight in the 880 and mile. I'm putting McIlrath in some other races." It was unspoken, but I realized he just eliminated my biggest competitor.

Once again, Dad stood proudly along the track and coached me from the sidelines. I ran my quarter mile of the mile relay, and we took first place. I ran the 880 run and placed first. Then, I ran the mile run, my favorite race. I felt great running, and with Dad cheering me down the home stretch of the last lap, I crossed the finish line in—first place! Dad and I were both jumping for joy after this race. I received three medals that night and enjoyed hearing my name announced over the loudspeaker for first place, but most of all, I was grateful to my dad, first for not giving up on finding a race for me to run, and then for not letting me quit. He deserved the gold medal that night.

My high-school years were filled with much happiness and other distractions besides running. I started dating my high-school sweetheart, John, during my sophomore year. He was tall, good-looking, smart, and a senior. He was also an athlete involved in football, basketball and track. He dominated my heart and thoughts. When I wasn't spending time with him, I was busy with other activities.

I did not train during the off-season. Instead, I stayed busy with student council meetings, softball, cheerleading practices, and the school newspaper. In my spare time, I worked at Anthony's Department Store on the town square.

The biggest distraction was boys. Before I met John, dating was a tricky thing for me. My father and two brothers were quite protective, to put it mildly. I tried pushing the limits a few times, but often it backfired on me, like the time I was told specifically by Dad my freshman year that I was not allowed to ride in a particular boy's car. Tony was known for his crazy driving habits. It would have spared me some embarrassment if only I had taken Dad's advice seriously.

However, temptation eventually overruled, if only for a few minutes. The car was a beautiful yellow convertible Mustang. My girlfriend and I were walking around town, when Tony pulled up and asked if we needed a ride. We didn't think twice about the offer before we leapt into the backseat. And about five blocks later, I would be leaping right back out.

The joy ride ended when a gold Ford LTD with a white top came roaring up behind us, blasting the horn and blinking the headlights on and off. The instant I turned my head, I knew who was behind us.

"Tony, pull over … pull over … stop the car! It's my dad."

The mention of my dad brought him to a screeching halt. I hopped out of the backseat and into the passenger side of my dad's car without hesitation. Few words were spoken on the ride home. There was no need. I could sense the disappointment in my dad's face.

The consequences for riding in that beautiful car: two-week grounding. To me, that seemed like eternity.

Dad had a reputation around town for his protectiveness of my sister and me. One night I was riding in Jim Schwartz-kopf's van—with permission, this time of course. Jim asked if anyone had a curfew, and I replied, "Mine is ten o'clock."

Jim quickly responded, "Then you are going home first, because I don't want Shot Gun Floyd coming after me!"

"What do you mean 'Shot Gun Floyd'? My dad doesn't even have a gun."

Jim laughed. "Didn't you know? That's what kids in town call your dad. It's because of his stern look and the way he peeks out the front door window, blinking the porch light off and on when a guy brings you home."

"No," I honestly replied, "I can't believe you would say that about my dad. He is the kindest man I know."

Jim was not convinced. He jokingly said, "You are still going home first, and I have ten minutes to get you there before the shotgun goes off."

As Jim pulled his van into my driveway, the porch light was already on, but when the top of my dad's head appeared in the window, and the light started blinking, I knew that was my cue to get out of the van. It was then that I fully understood what Jim meant.

That was not the most embarrassing moment I had breaking Dad's rules. The ultimate offense was an incident at the Lake of the Ozarks in Missouri. It has been referred to as "Sue's purple hat escapade." And over the years, I have been reminded about it more times than I care to discuss.

Every summer we traveled to the Lake of the Ozarks for a week of family vacation. One summer we were privileged to stay at Kon Tiki Resort, a beautiful waterfront resort with many kids our age, especially boys.

A tall, blond, curly-haired guy named Charlie caught my eye immediately. Luckily for me, my brother buddied up with him for the week. Randy was always gracious when it came to letting his sister tag along. And was I ever thankful he let me tag along this time. It didn't take long to sense the attraction between Charlie and me. He was fourteen, and I was thirteen.

We became boyfriend and girlfriend for the week. It basically meant swimming and talking together every day and evening—except for one evening.

My parents had given each one of us a curfew depending on our age and gender. In my mind, the curfews were not fair. My brothers always got to stay out much later, just because they were boys.

Our vacation was ending in three days. That evening, several kids from the resort planned to meet at the boat dock to hang out on our parents' boat, listening to music and talking. My dad had set my curfew at 10:00 P.M. My brother's curfew was 11:30 P.M. I argued the case like an attorney with my parents about how unjust this was. They didn't budge and reminded me that I was wasting valuable time arguing.

So I accepted the curfew and joined everyone down on the boat dock for a few hours of fun. When the clock struck ten and my dad flipped the outside porch light off and on, I knew my time was up. Begrudgingly, I said my good-byes, and then whispered in Charlie's ear, "I might be back."

I went promptly to the bedroom assigned to me and my sister, Sheila, who was already sleeping in the bed we were sharing. I knew my parents would turn in shortly after the news on TV, so I waited for about thirty minutes before I executed my plan.

The plan included stuffing my side of the bed with clothes from my suitcase to imitate my sleeping body. That proved to be the easy part.

Shaping a head was more challenging. Fortunately, the night before, I had purchased a lovely purple-felt floppy hat as a memento of the trip. The purple hat was ideal. I stuffed it with a towel and positioned it on the pillow. My decoy was complete. I was quite pleased as I pulled the blanket over my creation.

My sister slept through the entire project and didn't so much as wiggle on her side of the bed. I was so proud of myself.

Quietly, I left the condo and headed straight for the boat dock. When I appeared out of the darkness, everyone looked shocked—especially my brother Randy.

"Sue, do Dad and Mom know you're here?" he asked.

"Nope, and don't worry, they won't wake up. Besides, if they do wake up and check the room, it will look like I'm there. I made a dummy in the bed with clothes and my purple hat."

"You better hope Dad doesn't wake up to do a bed check."

Then Charlie's friend, Roger, responded with words I still remember.

"If your dad comes walking down that boat ramp, I am going to be like Jesus and walk on water," he said.

My freedom lasted for about twenty minutes. That's when the condo lights blasted on like the great shining on the seventh day. Within seconds, Dad appeared at the end of the boat dock with a strut like a four-star general.

Randy took one look at Dad. "We all better start walking on water."

I bolted from the boat and headed toward my dad, embarrassed and afraid of what he was going to say.

"Get up to the condo." Then he paused. "Sue," he said.

"Yes," I sheepishly answered.

"Your camouflage almost worked, except then your sister rolled over, and there was your purple hat."

The consequences for foolishness are never fun. That little outing cost me: I was grounded for the rest of the trip. I was able to go to the pool during the day, but I was confined to the condo for the evenings.

I didn't spend *all* of my high school days grounded. The happiest moment during this period occurred my senior year during homecoming week. I was nominated as a candidate for homecoming queen.

It was a thrill to be nominated. I must admit, to buy a new formal dress added to the excitement. Mom and I shopped at Younker's Department Store in Des Moines and found the perfect dress. It was a beautiful high-collared, sleeveless coral dress with a matching hooded jacket.

Homecoming week in Adel was always jam-packed with activities, with the finale on Friday. In the afternoon, the annual homecoming parade made its way through town and ended on the town square with skits and introduction of the homecoming queen candidates.

The football game followed at 7:00 PM in the park. At half-time, the queen was announced.

That particular night was picture-perfect. It was somewhat chilly but still tolerable without a coat. The sky was clear and bursting with bright stars everywhere. The cheerleaders had our hometown crowd in a craze of cheering and chanting.

At half-time, each candidate was driven in a car around the entire football field so we could wave at the fans. It was a dream car—a convertible that I actually had permission to ride in this time.

I spotted my entire family and boyfriend John in the bleachers. They were easy to spot. Dad was standing and waving wildly.

I was the last to be introduced to the crowd. Coach Bond, a science teacher and wrestling coach, was asked to crown the queen.

I was shocked when the announcer said the 1976 Homecoming Queen for Adel-DeSoto High School was—Sue Seibert! I immediately looked up at my family. They were ecstatic, and so was I! You might say it was a race I didn't think I could win. But I did.

Overall, my days spent in high school were quite memorable. High school was filled with struggles, losses, and triumphs.

My dream was to be a really great long-distance runner, but it didn't happen. Instead, I was a good runner who never gave up trying—thanks to my dad's coaching and encouragement.

I learned that everyone deals with defeat at some time. In retrospect, the defeat I experienced on the track taught me about life. Life is unpredictable. It really doesn't matter what place you end up as long as you finish the race you are asked to run.

Fifth Race:
Looking Ahead

Running is the greatest metaphor of life, because you get out of it what you put into it.

Oprah Winfrey

No one can prepare you for your first experience of leaving home.

I had anticipated this day since spring of my senior year. In fact, several times when I was feeling particularly mature and independent, I announced to my family that I could not wait to be out on my own.

Fall of 1977 was an entirely new race in life for me to run. I was enrolled at Iowa State University in Ames, Iowa.

Dad had the duty of packing the car with all my belongings. By the time he was finished, only the front seat of the car remained empty. Dad could not go along because of his on-call work schedule; however, Mom was more than willing to drive me to college for the big event. I was truly blessed with a mother who was available for me throughout life, too, just like Dad had been. She and I have always had, and continue to have, a close relationship. In fact, many times I've told friends, mom is my best friend. We talk about anything. Well, almost anything.

I was assigned to live on the seventh floor in Maple Hall, referred to as "heaven on seventh." The dormitory had eight floors in total and two sets of elevators. We were looking forward to using those elevators to haul my stuff up to the room.

The moment we drove into the parking lot, I sensed something was wrong. Cars and trucks were parked every which way. No one appeared to be using the front doors. Instead, the side doors were propped open, and people were carrying loads of their belongings up the stairs. The elevators had broken down.

At that point, I sure could have used Dad's help, but within minutes after finding a parking place and making one exhausting trip up the stairs, the lifesavers came to the rescue.

Steve Fisher and Jim Peters were "Adel boys." They were older than me by a couple of years and lived in a fraternity house off campus. Thankfully, they happened to be cruising by in a convertible with some other fraternity brothers at just the right time. Their objective for this drive-by was to scope out the new arrivals for fall. And this new arrival desperately needed their help.

Poor guys! When they so graciously jumped out and offered to help, I don't think they realized how much stuff was packed into our car. The temperature that day was close to 100 degrees, with heavy humidity.

They were real troopers and made several trips before the job was completed. My mom offered to pay them because she was so grateful for their help. They declined and went off to help other girls in distress.

Mom settled me in to my new dormitory room, and then suggested we run out and get a bite to eat before she returned home.

Upon arriving back at the dormitory, we said our good-byes. We were both teary-eyed. Mom reiterated the fact that she and Dad were very proud of me for attending Iowa State University. Her last comment that evening stuck in my memory: "I love you, and you can call us any time."

As her car pulled away, and I was left standing alone on the sidewalk with the towering dormitory behind me, I didn't feel so great. In fact, it felt like my stomach would combust. It was my second real experience with homesickness. The excited young girl who was seeking freedom wanted to run after that car and scream, "Don't leave me here!"

The only other time I had been away from my parents for an extended period of time was when I went to church camp at the age of twelve. It did not go well.

I had only been at camp for an hour when I asked to go home. The head camp counselor said empathetically that they didn't let kids go home unless they were sick.

I started to cry and cried all day long, hoping that would convince them to let me go home. It didn't. Over the next several days, I wrote many letters begging my parents to come pick me up. That didn't work either.

By midweek, the camp counselors didn't know what to do with me. They finally allowed me to eat all of my meals with my brother Randy, who was also attending the camp. In the evenings I was permitted to sit by him again around the camp-fire.

He gave me several heart-to-heart pep talks and reassured me that camp would be fun. "But," he begged, "you have to quit crying!"

By the end of the week, the tears had dried up, and I found solace in counting the hours until my parents would pick me up on Saturday morning. And when their gold Ford pulled into the parking lot … well, let's just say it was one of those hallelujah moments!

However, my first day on campus was not an hallelujah moment. This meant four years away at college and an hour away from my family.

I headed immediately for that stairwell and ran up those seven flights of stairs to make a call to my dad to tell him that Mom was on her way home. (It was a family ritual whenever one of our family members traveled.) When Dad answered, I tried to remain upbeat. Of course, I told him all about the chaos and broken-down elevators.

"So what do you think about your dorm room? Have you met any of the girls on the floor yet?"

My upbeat voice cracked, and I broke down. "I don't think I'm going to like this. Everything seems too big, and I want to come home."

Dad responded in his reassuring, loving way. "Sue, you just got there. You will be fine once your roommate comes and you start classes. It will be OK, honey. You can come home on the weekends if you want. You are only an hour away. I will have your mom call you as soon as she gets home."

He continued. "And Sue ... keep running. It will help you feel better. I love you. Bye."

So that is exactly what I did. I put on my running gear and took off to explore my new home away from home.

The homesickness lasted for the entire first quarter. I phoned my parents many times in those three long months to discuss quitting school. My phone bill was astronomical, but I didn't care. I just wanted them to tell me it would be fine to quit and move home. However, they did not. Instead, they coached me through the emotional ordeal and would by no means allow me to quit. Dad said I needed to give it a year. He promised me that by spring, I would be happier.

Parents are amazing at predicting some things. By spring I had indeed fallen in love with college life. I stopped going home on the weekends and started socializing like everyone else. In fact, I even looked forward to returning in the fall for my sophomore year.

The second year of college brought more choices—like whether or not to live in a sorority house. Some of my friends from my freshman year had joined sororities and loved them. It appeared to me to be such a family environment. And I was all for family, so I entertained the notion of going through the rush process to join a sorority.

The week-long process of rush can be a very emotional and downright scary experience. Initially, you visit all the sororities. Then you decide which ones you would like to go back to, while the sororities are also making their selections. As the week progresses, you narrow your choices down to two houses—your first and second choices—then wait and hope you'll be matched into one of them. It doesn't always work out, though. A mismatch can occur, which simply means you did not get in a house. For the most part, everyone is placed and ends up relatively happy. I know for me that was certainly true. The Gamma Phi Beta Sorority was the one I had hoped and prayed would like me. Luckily, my prayers were answered, and I became a Gamma Phi Beta pledge in the fall of 1978.

During rush week, I met many girls from my sorority. The girls who made the biggest impression on me were three girls from West Des Moines. Cathy, Carol, and Roxanne were genuine, energetic, beautiful blondes. I called them the "Valley Girls." Ironically, they had attended Valley High School in West Des Moines. Their high school had been one of our rivals during track season. All three ran track. I recalled them as sprinters. They remembered me as a long-distance runner. We became instant friends.

Sorority life provided many opportunities for meeting boys. Meeting young men was always on the forefront of my mind or any college girl's mind. Dates were not as abundant for me as they were for some of my friends. However, occasionally a guy would ask me out on a date or to a party. Some were fun to be around, though on more than one occasion I went on dates that couldn't end soon enough.

There was one guy with whom I was wildly infatuated. I just knew my parents would have the same feeling once they met Dave, so I invited him to Adel.

After this introduction, I asked my dad what he thought of the new boyfriend. His initial response was not what I had expected.

His exact words went like this: "Sue, that young man wouldn't cut the grass if it grew up around his knees." It was my dad's way of saying—he had no ambition.

One month later, Dave and I were discussing life after college. He said that he would like to move to Colorado and live off the land. I wanted to live in a city with a career in social work, which was my major. Shortly after this conversation, the relationship ended.

During my junior year, I received some crushing news about Dad. It was January 1980, and Mom had phoned to tell me that Dad had been diagnosed with lung cancer. Earlier that week he had coughed blood. His physician found cancer cells in his right lung and scheduled surgery for the following week. I immediately made plans to leave college and return home for a week to be with him and the rest of my family.

Dad's surgery was performed at Mercy Hospital in Des Moines. He came through the surgery fine but was rescheduled for another surgery that same week. The physician said he didn't remove all the cancerous tissue the first time. The second surgery was performed to remove the remaining part of the right lung. Overall, Dad was in good physical shape, so he survived the second surgery. And no chemotherapy or radiation was needed after the surgeries.

The entire ordeal was very emotional for me. I hated seeing my dad in intensive care with all the tubes connected to the machines. I was afraid he was going to die. The thought of losing my dad was inconceivable to me. My mom reassured me that he would pull through, and he did.

Dad experienced a period of depression after the surgery, which is not uncommon. He was concerned that the cancer was still present somewhere in his body. My mom provided the support and encouragement he needed to ease his concern. She also prayed a lot. So did I.

During his recuperation, we had many discussions. Dad's cancer was caused from smoking. He started smoking when he went off to play baseball for the farm club. He said it was something he did because everyone else was doing it. He didn't realize how addictive it had become. He kept repeating how he wished he had never started smoking. After the cancer, he never considered lighting another cigarette. He also encouraged other people to quit so they wouldn't end up like him. I confessed to him that I had tried smoking a few cigarettes in college. He urged me to stop. I finally did after a few failed attempts.

Dad's follow-up tests cleared him of any further signs of cancer. It eased his mind and the depression. He soon felt strong and returned to work. Going back to work was therapeutic for him. I was back at school and decided to run more on a regular basis. The running helped me feel good and focus on my studies in social work.

A few of us from the sorority enjoyed going to the gym around 10:00 PM to run on the indoor track. This late outing had several objectives. First and foremost it was to exercise, to keep in shape. Secondly, it gave us a burst of energy so we could return to the house for late-night studying. Thirdly, and most important, we went to check out the boys.

A group of athletes caught our eyes. They happened to be members of the Iowa State wrestling team. The attraction to these boys was not just their good looks and toned physiques but what they drove—motorcycles!

I'm not sure if we liked them or their cycles more. However, the spring of 1980 proved to be one of the best times in my life.

One of the more memorable moments was the time a couple of wrestlers decided to use the hill in the front yard of the sorority house as a practice ramp for their motorcycles. I'm not sure what was worse: the actual stunt, or the time of day in which they decided to pull it.

Eleven-thirty at night may seem late to some people but not for college students. This time of night is still considered early, a time when students are out partying or just beginning to study. This particular night, many of my sorority sisters were in the main dining hall cramming for midterms. The dining hall was an absolutely beautiful room located on ground level, encased by a wall of windows overlooking the front yard.

The sudden revving of motorcycle engines was enough to startle everyone out of their studies. As the motorcycles flew by the windows, Roxanne and I knew exactly who the culprits were. Our unspoken expressions betrayed our emotions: we knew we too were in big trouble.

Consequently, the next morning a few of the wrestling groupies were summoned to see the house mother—Mom Behm. Thankfully, she was a fun-spirited person and had mercy on us. However, she had us relay a message to the boys on the bikes. "Tell 'Hot Wheels' the front yard is off limits for future stunts."

My senior year was consumed with completing my studies in social work. Even though I enjoyed my senior year both academically and socially, I was anxious, like any senior, to graduate and explore the working world. Another race in life you must run.

Graduation day finally arrived. My parents assured me that they would be there, along with my oldest brother, Denny, and his wife, Tresa. My sister and other brother were living in Arizona at the time and could not make the trip back.

The graduation ceremony was held at Hilton Coliseum, which hosted all the major indoor events. Even with a building capacity of 15,000, there were very few vacant seats that day.

As I sat in my chair on the floor of Hilton Coliseum, I reflected on all the events I had attended there. There were memories of watching basketball games, wrestling meets, and graduation ceremonies of friends. The huge highlight of the entire four years was being asked to attend the Billy Joel concert with Cathy Dugan and her cute brother, Brian.

However, on this day, the graduates were all seated in row after row on the main floor. The guests surrounded us on all sides. Looking up at all those people gave me an overwhelming feeling of exhilaration and accomplishment.

I told my parents that there was no way I would see them at this ceremony since there was no assigned seating. The game plan was to meet up with them at the Gamma Phi Beta House for the reception honoring the seniors.

Minutes before the ceremony was to take place, my friend Francy, who was a sorority sister and sitting next to me, grabbed my arm. "Look, Sue, there's your dad up there. They're waving at you."

At first, I saw only a mass of people sitting way up in the upper deck. "I don't see him."

Francy clasped her hands around my head and directed my eyes to a man sitting on the edge of his seat waving one arm back and forth from the upper bleachers. I couldn't believe I was able to spot him in this crowd. It was definitely my proud dad. To acknowledge him, I jumped up and waved back frantically with both arms.

It dawned on me that no matter what I accomplished in life, my dad was always along the sidelines somewhere, encouraging me to finish—finish the race that I had set out to run. And he was proud of me for enduring the race no matter what place I finished in. However, this day, I felt like I had won a big race, and so had Dad. He was healthy again and at my graduation. I had com-

pleted four years of college with a bachelor's degree in social work. And I was ready to save the world.

Sixth Race:
Stepping outside the Lane

Do what you can, with what you have, where you are.

Theodore Roosevelt

In the spring of my senior year of college, I had reunited with my high-school sweetheart, John. We went steady through high school and had parted ways in college to date others. He was now living and working in Wichita, Kansas.

My original plan was to move to Kansas City, Missouri, to live and work. I loved this city and imagined myself living there after graduation. However, I was having a heck of a time finding a job in social work. And without a job, I could not save the world or even pay rent.

Instead, John convinced me to change my mind and move to Wichita. He thought if we lived in the same town, we could start dating on a more serious level. And he was willing to make some contacts for possible job opportunities. He didn't have to twist my arm too hard to get me to agree. I had never stopped loving him and was thrilled he was back in my life.

So I headed south—approximately seven hours from Adel.

My parents were supportive and helped me make the big move. I stumbled upon a small, and I mean small, one-bedroom apartment to set up as my very first home away from home.

It was a newly constructed apartment complex close to everything I would need. Dad made sure I was on the second floor and the door had a strong deadbolt. He even talked, or shall we say interviewed, my next-door male neighbor. Dad gave his approval. He paid my first two months of rent plus the deposit. Then we headed to the grocery to stock my pantry and refrigerator.

Right before he and Mom were to leave me there all alone in a new city and a new apartment, he handed me a roll of cash.

"Tuck this in a sock and hide it away in a drawer. You might need this extra money some day," he whispered.

I glanced at the roll of money and immediately stuffed it into my jean pocket.

The time finally came when we had to say our good-byes, something I was dreading. Deep down inside I was scared, but I tried to pretend that I could handle this move. Dad went over some last-minute advice, ending with a word of caution.

"Sue, you be careful running alone. Never run in secluded places. And never at night." I promised Dad I would be careful.

As their car pulled away from the parking lot for the trip back to Iowa, both waved furiously, with Dad honking the horn until he pulled out on the main road and drove out of sight. Then the feeling returned—not as bad as what I had at camp or college—but nonetheless, that familiar feeling of homesickness stirred in my stomach.

As I headed up the steps to my new apartment, I decided to check the roll of bills that Dad had slipped me. When I counted it, my eyes filled with tears. He had given me $650. At this time in my life, I felt rich.

The job hunting in social work wasn't as easy as I'd imagined it would be. The job market had an overabundance of social workers and very few openings. Therefore, I resorted to plan "B": take any reasonable job offer, just to have a paycheck.

My work experience in high school and college consisted of retail sales and cleaning homes. I decided to pursue retail. My efforts landed me a job the first week I hit the pavement. Henry's Department Store was my first employer.

The sales clerk job supported me for a while, but my extra cash was disappearing quickly. Being on my own was a learning experience. It was the first time I understood the meaning of the word "budget."

On my days off, I searched for social work jobs. I was determined to find something in my profession. I couldn't imagine working as a sales clerk forever. Plus, I needed more income.

Out of desperation one day, I stopped at a Residence Inn to see if they needed any part-time office help. They were well staffed in that area. So I inquired about cleaning rooms. At that point, the receptionist, a caring older woman, questioned why a college-educated person would want to clean rooms.

"Honestly," I admitted, "I need to make more money, or I will have to move back to Iowa and live with my parents. I'll do almost anything to make some extra cash."

She told me she needed some time to think about it before she could make a decision.

Approximately one hour later, my phone rang. I used the "let it ring three times" tactic. I did not want whoever was calling to think I was anxiously sitting by the phone, which, of course, I was.

It was the woman from the Inn, saying she might know of a job in social work of interest to me. I couldn't believe what I was hearing.

"Do you remember seeing the man painting the walls when you walked into the office?"

"Yes," I responded.

"Well, he overheard our conversation and felt bad that you were having a tough time finding a social work job. He told me that he thinks there is an opening in the court services department in Eldorado, Kansas, which is only twenty minutes from here."

She encouraged me to call the courthouse to get more details about the job.

The minute the phone disconnected, I was calling directory assistance for Butler County Courthouse.

It was my lucky day. My call was forwarded to the court administrator, Steve. He was very congenial and said they had not been pleased with the applicants, and the job was still vacant. We discussed my education and volunteer experience. He asked me to send him my resume. I sent it that same day!

The painter had been a true blessing. Within two weeks of that encounter, I was employed as a court services officer for Butler County. Neal Harrison was my supervisor—another blessing. He was an intuitive man who realized I was a nice but very naïve small-town girl from Iowa who needed some exposure to real life situations, some of which would prove to be horrific.

I would finally learn that growing up in a small town—combined with being raised in a very loving, protective family—was not the real world. Growing up, I'd only had glimmers of the real world through my dad, who would tell me of families that were poor and couldn't pay their electric or gas bills on time, if at all.

On many occasions Dad confided in me about these troubling circumstances. The conversations typically followed this dialogue.

"I just couldn't turn off my customers' electricity or gas today," he would comment.

"So what did you do?"

"I made a note that I didn't have time to go and would go on Friday."

"Why on Friday?" I questioned.

"Because most people get paid on Fridays, and hopefully they can pay their bill before I have to go back out to their house and turn off anything."

My dad always held on to the hope that giving them an extra day or so would somehow bring a payment. Sometimes it did and sometimes, well, it didn't. And then he would have to perform the inevitable task he so hated.

Another heart-tugging experience for him was being called to work in a part of Des Moines after thunderstorms ripped through town and left downed power lines. The area at that time was called the "South Bottoms," a place stricken with severe poverty. It disturbed him to see the conditions some children and adults were living in. On several occasions when Dad felt his children needed a gentle reminder of their blessings, he would load us into the car and drive us through this neighborhood. He didn't have to say anything. We got the message loud and clear. *Be thankful you have a warm, well-built home. Be thankful you have food, clothes, toys, and a car.*

I learned a lot from these trips. There really are people in our country who cannot meet their basic needs. And if we can, we should help them. Dad's actions spoke louder than his words in so many ways.

Little did I know the new job I was about to embark on was most certainly going to expose me to those in need of many things. Neal eased me gently into this new world of stark reality. At first, I was assigned juveniles who had committed minor offenses. The crimes most often included truancy from school or shoplifting at the local five-and-dime store. My youngest case was a six-year-old who became my favorite client. When Rex and his mother walked into my office, I thought to myself, *There has to be a big mistake here.*

To begin with, he was small for his age. He must have inherited his small stature from his petite mother. He was dressed in his Sunday best and was very scared. I tried putting him at ease by smiling a lot and sitting next to him and not behind the desk. When I read the police report, I realized he was being accused of stealing a bicycle. I asked Rex to tell me his side of the story.

He gave this account. "My mom sent me to the store by my house to buy bread. When I came out of the store, I saw a bicycle, so I rode it home." End of story.

His mother then chimed in and told me how the police came out to their house and took Rex to the police station to question him.

At that point, I excused myself, rushed over to Neal's office, and shut the door behind me. (He had one of those open-door policies unless you really needed to talk to him about a private matter. I considered this to be one of those private matters.)

I immediately blurted out, "Neal, have you seen that little boy in my office? He is six years old. His feet don't come anywhere close to touching the floor. I can't put this little guy on probation. Mom doesn't have the time or money to drive him over here every week. This is ridiculous."

Before I could say any more, Neal interrupted my passionate plea. "Calm down, Sue. I agree with you. I'm not sure why this ever made it this far. Let Rex know that it was wrong for him to take the bike. Tell them that there will *not* be any probation recommended and *not* to ride anyone's bike unless he asks. And you do not want to see him in this office again." So that is exactly what I did. And out the door went a relieved little six-year-old and a grateful mother.

Juvenile offenders were next on my caseload, which opened my eyes even wider. They were mainly boys who enjoyed stealing the bigger items, like cars, or breaking into and entering businesses. I always felt sorry for these kids and hoped somehow the probation would help them get their lives back on the right path. Some successfully completed their probation work. Others failed and were sent off to internment facilities for juvenile offenders. I hated making that recommendation.

Then came something that I truly dreaded: child abuse cases. These cases literally made my heart ache, and in some instances, made me sick to my stomach.

Child abuse and neglect are things I could not fathom and will never fully understand as long as I live. Yes, I was disciplined as a child. I received a few spankings. More often, I lost privileges when I misbehaved. That is where it should stop. No slapping on the face. No hitting with the hand or object on the head or body. No emotional or mental abuse.

Linda was the Butler County case worker assigned to investigate the alleged child abuse and neglect cases. She invited me to attend a meeting to discuss some allegations against a mother and her live-in boyfriend. I was forewarned about the pictures I might see. However, no one could have prepared me for what I viewed. It nauseated me. On the way back to the office, I asked Linda how anyone could have children live in those horrible conditions or do the things allegedly done to them.

"I can't explain why anyone would choose to beat or neglect their children. For some it is a vicious cycle. They were mistreated as children, and that's all they know. Somehow the cycle *must* be broken, because no child deserves to be brought into this world to be abused or neglected."

The court services office was always notified when there was a hearing for child abuse and neglect. Someone had to attend from our office. At one point, I sat directly behind a man who had sexually abused a two-year-old. It was hard for me to remain silent in the face of this despicable person.

These cases I observed made me feel helpless at times because I did not have the authority to change the situation. But for many years, I prayed for those children. I prayed that God would protect them from any future harm.

Adult offenders were next on my learning agenda. Neal was selective in which cases were added to my caseload. I began to view Neal as an extension of my father's protective arm.

One day, Neal asked if I would like to accompany him on an interview for a pre-sentence report with an alleged murderer of a Kansas highway patrolman. My exact thought: *I'm sure glad they asked him and not me.* Even though I was reluctant at first, he encouraged me to tag along. So I did.

Before we entered the jail, Neal went over the game plan of what would occur. "Don't let this guy intimidate or scare you."

"OK," I said as I clutched my fists tightly and took a deep breath. But Neal's parting advice went right out the window the second the police officer escorted the shackled man into the small room. I think "scared to death" was written all over my face the instant I made eye contact with him. He immediately realized I was petrified. He took advantage of the situation and stared at me with an intensity that, to my frightened mind, seemed to radiate evil—a look I had never witnessed in my twenty-two years.

Neal handled the interview in a calm and professional manner. He was a former Marine; nothing appeared to rattle him. I, on the other hand, sat like a stone statue, huddling as close as I could get to Neal without making him feel too uncomfortable.

It was an event that changed how I viewed life. My secure upbringing had not prepared me for certain experiences. After the trial and the jury convicted the man of murder, I learned another reality in life. Evil really does exist. Had I reached across the table that day during the pre-sentence visit, I could have touched it.

My first job in the field of social work was an eye-opener for a small-town girl from Iowa. The experience was invaluable. I learned about the good and the bad in life. I also learned a lot about myself. That, as a social worker, I needed to view the world we live in as complex with many problems. Sometimes you have to step outside your lane and understand the difficult races others have to run. Unfortunately, though, after a year I resigned. The decision was actually bittersweet. I was leaving the area because I had a better offer. The offer was a proposal from my first love, John. And the offer included change.

The change in my life not only involved going from Miss to Mrs., it meant a move to another state. I took a leap of faith and agreed to the marriage and the move.

Seventh Race:
True Commitment

What lies behind us and what lies before us are tiny matters compared to what lies within us.

Ralph Waldo Emerson

The fairytale wedding that I had dreamed about since I was a little girl took place on June 5, 1982, in Des Moines, Iowa, at St. Mark's Lutheran Church. It was a large wedding with family and friends traveling from around the Midwest.

Naturally, my dad was given the privilege of walking me down the aisle to give me away. You wonder what really goes through a father's mind at this moment. But I do know one thing—my father had treated me with so much love and respect that I'm sure that's what he hoped for in my husband.

Dad looked so handsome in his tuxedo that day. He appeared to have a glow just like me. I'm sure this came from being proud that he could give his daughter the wedding of her dreams. Dad had given my mom and me a nice budget for the wedding. It wasn't outrageously extravagant, but to me the day was perfect—from the ceremony to the reception at the country club.

As Dad and I waited for the music that would herald my grand entrance, we stood back in the narthex of the church and talked quietly. Mainly he was trying to calm my nerves. My legs were feeling a little wobbly, and he assured me I was not going to faint or trip.

"Just take a deep breath, hold onto my arm, and walk down the aisle. Everything will be just fine," he reassured me in his fatherly manner. Similar advice he had given me from my good old track days.

Then Dad got a little sentimental. He complimented me on my beauty as a bride and told me how proud he was of me as his daughter.

He continued speaking in his tender way. "Life goes by so quickly, Sue. It seems like yesterday that you were that little girl playing carefree in the backyard, swinging and singing on the swing set and digging in the sandbox."

Dad concluded our memorable conversation with a wishful statement.

"I hope your marriage will be as happy as your mother's and mine has been. Your mom was the best thing that ever happened to me."

"Dad, I love John so much. We will have a good marriage, too."

"I hope so, honey," he responded with a smile.

When my dad mentioned his marriage to me that day, I could see the love by the gleam in his eyes and the smile he could not contain when he spoke of Mom.

My parents met at Lake Robbins Ballroom in Perry, Iowa, during a dance. It was love at first sight by both accounts. The courtship evolved into a strong marriage founded on a true commitment to one another. It had all the right ingredients for a successful marriage—love, respect, and trust.

My parents took their vows of marriage very seriously. As far back as I can recall, they loved and adored each other. They also communicated well. It seemed they were always discussing something of importance. And I think sometimes it was the simple, selfless acts they conscientiously performed that kept their love for one another so passionate over many years.

Mom enjoyed cooking Dad's favorite meals. She bought all his clothes. Dad thought she had great fashion sense. She regularly planned a date night to go dancing at the ballroom where they met. She constantly voiced her love for him and spoke proudly about his hard work and providing for the family. And she wrote him love notes.

Dad's kindness showed in numerous ways, too. He complimented Mom often about her appearance, cooking, and mothering skills. He always made sure her car was filled with gas, and during the winter months, he would warm it up before she drove it. He helped around the house without being asked. He frequently folded a load of clothes or placed a roast in the oven before joining us at church on Sunday. And he had no problem showing his affection for her. I witnessed him many times coming home after work giving her a kiss or grabbing her for a quick dance around the kitchen. And he wrote her love notes.

He thoroughly delighted in buying gifts for her. And it became a tradition for him to take me and my sister along on these special buying trips. Certain shopping sprees still stand out in my mind.

Eckerman Jewelry Store was located on the town square in Adel. It was a typical jewelry store filled with shiny glass display cases of gems just waiting to be discovered. On this particular trip we were hunting for a new fashion watch for Mom. After several were pulled from the glass case and lined up for careful examination by my dad, my sister, and me, we selected a gold watch with cut diamonds set along the sides of the square face.

Dad excitedly reached for his wallet to pay for the watch. He politely asked the clerk to wrap it up. "Your mom will be so surprised when we give this to her." Dad truly enjoyed shopping for gifts for his wife.

This experience was just the beginning of what I learned from him about giving from a loving heart.

Christmas was always a joyous time in our household. Dad typically worked many more hours of overtime due to power outages caused by the snow storms that would blast the Midwest region in December. Overtime meant more presents under the tree and a big family dinner with all the relatives.

Dad put a lot of thought into gifts for Mom, and again would always take Sheila and me along. I remember the

Christmas he took us again down to the town square to shop for a present. We ended up at Bernadine's.

It was no secret in town that Bernadine's was known for its classic, beautiful clothing and expensive price tags.

Obviously, Dad had some good overtime this year because he wanted to buy Mom a nightgown and matching robe. We browsed through the racks together until Bernadine herself assisted us.

We settled on a long, beautiful off-white, silky, sleeveless gown with a matching velour robe trimmed in aqua satin. Sheila and I gave Dad our stamp of approval. "Mom will look so beautiful in that." Dad smiled in agreement.

I accompanied my dad on many shopping excursions over the years to help choose the perfect gift for Mom's birthday or Christmas. And every year his love for her was reflected in his genuine thoughtfulness and enthusiasm.

He also had some yearly traditions that he never forgot—the Easter lily for Easter and the poinsettia at Christmas. I can still picture his shining smile as he walked through the door making the special delivery. On Valentine's Day, he would buy a very large, heart-shaped box of chocolates for Mom, and then give us kids a smaller one. He never missed a year.

My parents set a good example of working at their marriage. They were dedicated to each other. That dedication included lots of love, communication, and acts of kindness.

I wanted our marriage to be just like my parents'. In some ways it emulated theirs. John and I were compatible in many areas. We enjoyed dancing, participating in sports, going to church, and socializing with other couples. We were very affectionate toward one another.

In other areas we struggled. Like many young couples, John and I had our share of disagreements and difficulties while trying to blend our unique backgrounds and personalities. John worked a lot, which left me alone and resentful at times. I didn't like the way he was so attentive to other women. He was thrifty. By contrast, I appeared to be a spendthrift. During our sixth year of marriage we sought marriage counseling. Thankfully, the counselor gave practical advice to help us get our marriage back on the right track.

I learned a lot about marriage from watching my parents through the years. They made it look so easy. But in reality, they put a lot of time and work into it. Just like running a race, to be good at marriage you must be dedicated and have an equally devoted partner who runs the race with you.

I practiced many of the things learned from my parents and the counselor in my marriage. I was committed to my husband and wanted this to work out. Now I was ready for the next challenge—children!

Eighth Race:
Cultivating Talents

Your talent is God's gift to you. What you do with it is your gift back to God.

Leo Buscaglia

Parenting is one of the most important races you will be asked to run. Unfortunately, there is no pre-season. You hit the ground running once that little bundle of joy arrives. The long course of this race will test your skills of patience, courage, strength, and endurance. And, like any good race run, it will be mixed with some victories and losses.

Having children caused me to reflect even more on my own childhood. I was reminded of the influence Dad had been on my life. He had put his heart and soul into being a good role model for his own children and other children as well. He believed every child had talent and should strive to discover and use it.

The moment I held our first daughter, Sara, on March 29, 1989, I realized the meaning of a miracle. I also understood more fully my dad's comment, "Some day you will be a parent and understand parents' love for their child." And when two more daughters were added to the equation, the love just multiplied. Anna was born on Thanksgiving Eve of November 27, 1991. Our youngest, Maria, was born on October 28, 1993.

There are Bible verses spoken often about love. A particular portion of a verse comes to mind from 1 Corinthians 13:4a, "Love is patient, love is kind."

Dad's parenting style must have been fashioned from that verse. It was evident in his persistent ways when cultivating my abilities and talents. No matter what he was trying to teach me, he did not give up until I got it right—which required a lot of patience!

Like the summer of 1970, when I tried relentlessly to learn to water-ski. We were taking our annual family camping vacation. That year we traveled to Deer Valley Park at the Lake of the Ozarks in Missouri.

The Van Gundy family journeyed with us on this trip. Stanley and Elsie were close friends of my parents. They had three children who were extremely compatible with my brothers, sister, and me.

Dad and Stanley were determined that by the end of the week every child would be water-skiing. Of course, that included me.

The Van Gundy kids could already ski quite well. They had an advantage since they had owned a speed boat for a few years. It didn't take my two brothers or my sister long before they were popping right out of the water and skiing upright for some distance.

I, on the other hand, looked like a bobber on a string dragging behind the boat. On some attempts I felt as if I had ingested most of the lake. Not to mention the effect this pull had on my swim-suit bottoms. Half the time they ended up around my knobby little knees. And to make matters worse, my brothers had a blast pointing and laughing at me from the back of the boat. It was a dreadful experience.

After many—and I mean many—failed attempts, I wanted to quit. I was tired of trying. My arms ached from being jerked by the initial pull of the boat to get me up on the skis. And my ego was severely bruised. I was the only child who had not mastered the sport.

So I flat-out told Dad, "I don't like water-skiing, and there is no need to keep trying. I will never be able to get up out of the water."

But Dad didn't buy that excuse. He gently said, "Sue, you almost have it. After dinner, Stanley and I'll take you out by ourselves. We'll find a cove where the water is like glass. We *will* get you up on skis. You can do this. You will be water-skiing this week like the other kids."

I thought about it for a few hours and trusted Dad could help me accomplish this feat.

I remember the evening like it happened yesterday. Stanley steered, while Dad coached me from the back of the boat. The sun was starting to set, casting a luminous glare on the lake. The water was smooth like glass, just as Dad had promised.

After a few unsuccessful attempts, I popped right out of the water, and, to my surprise, stayed upright.

Dad and Stanley were as elated as I was. Stanley gave a congratulatory wave with one hand while keeping the other on the steering wheel. Dad clasped his hands above his head with an enormous smile as if to say, "Hooray! You did it, Sue!"

My impulse was to wave back. I let go of the tow rope with one hand, but before I could make a gesture I crashed head first into the lake. When my face finally surfaced my smile said it all—Victory at last!

A few days had passed since I had mastered the skill of water-skiing. I was feeling quite confident in my abilities. So, when Stanley asked who would like to ski to Bagnell Dam with him, I was the first and only one who volunteered.

Bagnell Dam was approximately eleven miles by boat from our campground. The dam area was a tourist trap. It was a strip of shops that had a little bit of something for everyone. There were restaurants, rides, and plenty of souvenir stores.

Stanley had cautioned me before everyone loaded into the boat that the trip would be a rough ride. To get to the dam we had to ski the main channel. The water would be choppy, and we would hit some big waves, especially if we passed by the large tourist boats. Dad, the driver of the boat, assured me that he would keep the boat to the side of the channel and I could quit anytime.

Even being forewarned, I still wanted to try. In my mind I told myself, *you can do this*. There was also a hidden agenda. I was going to prove to everyone, especially my brothers, that I could now water-ski.

The saying "riding out the storm" is exactly what it felt like. The waves were relentless. I seemed to disappear a few times behind the boat when the big tour boats passed and left a huge wake, but I held on for dear life. Even though my legs felt like rubber bands, I was not going to quit!

Stanley was an excellent skier and took the waves with grace. Often he would ski near me to see if I was OK. All I could do was nod yes. Then he would ask, "Do you want to keep going?" Another head nod with the yes motion.

We skied the entire way to Bagnell Dam that evening with no falls or wipeouts. Dad was jubilant when I crawled up the ladder into the boat with my legs now feeling like over-cooked spaghetti.

I was congratulated by everyone, including my brothers. I didn't want to let on that I was exhausted, so I smiled at everyone except my brothers. I stuck my tongue out at them. That was my way of saying, "*Ha ha, I did it!*" At least they never made fun of me again, that is, when it came to water-skiing.

It was obvious Dad enjoyed teaching his children new skills and techniques. Take for instance, something as mundane as catching night crawlers.

Mr. Bleau owned the bait-and-tackle shop called "Gladys" located on Highway Six. We could see the shop from our back window. One day, while Dad was buying worms for a fishing outing, Mr. Bleau made a business proposition. He asked if Dad and his two sons would be interested in catching worms for his business. He would pay one cent per worm, but he wanted whole worms, not broken ones.

Dad brought up the idea to my brothers at the dinner table that evening. My brothers were excited about the opportunity, mainly because they saw dollar signs flashing in front of their eyes. Back in the early 1970s, one cent meant a lot to a child. They were already mentally calculating the money. One hundred worms equaled one dollar; five hundred worms equaled five dollars. And on a good rainy night, each brother could easily pick up one thousand worms for a ten-dollar bill.

After dinner I told Dad I needed to talk to him in private. We went to the front porch and sat on the edge of the brick flower planter where every year Mom planted her red and white petunias. I related my feelings about the night-crawler scheme. I told Dad it wasn't fair that I was excluded. I begged him to let me in on the deal. He was a little hesitant at first, but after I batted my big, sad brown eyes a few times, he agreed to teach me how to catch them the proper way.

There is a technique to night-crawler hunting. You must spot them quickly with your flashlight and then grab gently and pull the slimy things from their holes in the ground. The tricky part is not breaking them in two before you have successfully captured them.

I tended to pull too hard. Dad was patient with me, though, and would show me over and over again how to pull them out whole.

I found great joy in night-crawler hunting with my dad and brothers and loved the money that I made from doing this unusual job. On a rainy night, I could readily pick up eight hundred worms for eight dollars. It made a nice down payment on a pair of jeans.

On a few occasions, Mr. Bleau said he was finding too many broken worms. Dad never implicated any particular child. He just worked alongside me more often, reiterating the proper technique for retrieving the worms.

Dad found great delight in teaching his children how to play anything that involved a ball. You name it, and he taught it. However, I think his favorite was showing us how to play baseball.

Many nights after a long day at work he would gather us in the yard to play catch. If the neighborhood kids saw us, they joined in and it became a game.

I preferred pitching to Dad. He worked with me a lot on pitching. I wasn't very fast, but he said the most important thing to learn initially was hitting the strike zone and not to worry about the speed. That I could do. Well, most of the time. A few times I sent the ball sailing into our neighbor's front yard when I tried putting some speed on it.

I wished I had remembered his words of instruction one day while I was playing catch in the backyard with my brother, Denny. After we tossed a few, I told him I wanted to pitch some balls. He was reluctant to agree because Mrs. Raymond's yard was adjacent to our property, and we both knew how she felt about children and throwing balls.

Mrs. Raymond, our neighbor, appeared to dislike children. She never smiled, so we just assumed she was mean. Every time we played in our front yard, she peered out through her metal blinds. If we accidentally threw a ball into her yard, she would rap hard on the window. Those raps would scare the living daylights out of us and send us running into the house.

Denny reminded me of what I already knew. It is more important to pitch slow and hit the strike zone. However, I got a little too big for my britches and decided that since I was hitting the strike zone fine, I would need some speed.

I gave my brother fair warning: "Get ready for this one."

And with that, I let it go. The ball sailed over my brother's head and outstretched glove. It continued over the beautifully blooming lilac bush and over the fence. And for the grand finale, it soared right smack through the window of Mrs. Raymond's storage shed.

At first, my brother and I stood frozen. Then Denny yelled at me, "Look what you did! I told you not to throw it fast. I am not going to take the blame for this one. It's all your fault!"

We immediately turned and ran toward our back door. My gut feeling at that very moment was *I'm in big trouble now.* Just as I headed up the back stairs, I heard the phone ring.

My mother answered. "Yes, Mrs. Raymond. I'm very sorry, Mrs. Raymond. Floyd and I have told the kids many times not to play ball in that spot by the lilac bush."

There was a long pause.

"I'll call Floyd and have him fix it as soon as he can. I'm really sorry the kids did this."

My mother hung up the phone and turned facing the back door where her two guilty children stood. She didn't have to tell us who was on the phone. We had heard the conversation through the screen door.

"You kids know better than that. Your dad and I have told you over and over not to play catch in that part of the yard."

I immediately spoke up and accepted the responsibility for breaking the window. I should have listened to my brother. We never played catch in that spot again.

Dad had the window fixed before the sun set that evening. He wasn't too upset at me. He just reiterated where the strike zone was located and said, "Sometimes things like this happen to teach us a lesson." Then he jokingly said, "The next time you want to pitch fast, find a different backstop besides Mrs. Raymond's storage shed."

Another invaluable skill Dad taught us was driving. Teaching a teenager to drive could test anyone's patience. My introduction to this rite of passage involved cruising around in wide-open fields with Dad. When he was convinced that I could handle driving on a road, I graduated to the graveled country roads near our house.

I tended to have a heavy foot, which he pointed out on several occasions. I blame the heavy foot on two things: amusement park rides and tooling around town with my older brother Denny.

Every summer, Riverview Amusement Park devoted one Saturday in July to Iowa Power and Light Company employees and their families. It was always one of the highlights of my summer. Dad would give each of us equal numbers of ride tickets and two treat tickets apiece. My treat tickets were always spent on pink cotton candy and a grape snow cone.

My favorite ride of all time was the bumper cars. I liked the independent feeling when I was behind the wheel, and I loved flooring the pedal to crash someone from behind. My next-favorite ride was the Wild Mouse. It was the scariest and fastest roller coaster. It sat on the outskirts of the park next to the river. On a couple of curves you had the illusion that you were going to go right off the turn into the water.

My rationale for placing some blame on Denny about my driving habits started when he began driving. When teenagers begin driving they volunteer to go anywhere at any time when asked by a parent. Denny eagerly volunteered to pick me up from church youth group on Sunday evenings.

I loved having my big brother pick me up in his hot-looking, "jacked up" blue Mustang. I was the envy of my friends. Often, we rode around before returning home.

My favorite season to be picked up was wintertime. Winter brought snow and ice, and that meant the parking lot of the Adel Sale Barn was prime for turning "donuts." A donut is achieved by flooring the accelerator for speed and then braking to make the car spin in circles until it comes to a stop on its own. My brother could make the car spin like a top! Sometimes, he allowed me behind the wheel to turn a few. I soon got the hang of it.

Those moments were quite thrilling for me. But I've also paid the price over the years for a few bad driving habits learned from that maneuver.

The heavy foot on the accelerator has cost me a lot of money in fines. And quite often when I take my car in for servicing, the technician comments, "You are really hard on your brakes."

Dad had a loving way of discussing his concerns about areas of my life that begged criticism. Even as an adult, he worried about my driving habits.

It was the summer of 1988. John and I had just moved into our first house in Oklahoma City. My parents had planned a trip to visit us. I had a long list ready for my dad to do around the house. There wasn't anything he couldn't fix. One item on the list was a refrigerator that was malfunctioning.

He knew exactly what needed to be done. He and I ventured out to run errands and pick up a piece for the refrigerator at the General Electric store located thirty minutes from our house.

About twenty minutes into the outing, he glanced over at me.

"Sue, do you always drive like this?"

"What do you mean?"

"Well," he said, "first, you are driving too fast. When you passed that car back there, I thought you were going to sideswipe it. And honey, you hit those brakes like there is no tomorrow."

I just grinned and with a chuckle replied, "I've never had a wreck."

I should have knocked on wood.

Approximately six months later, as I was driving home from work during an ice storm, I hit the brakes too hard, went into a donut spin, and ended up in a ditch. I was fine physically but was emotionally shaken up over the ordeal. The car sustained major damage.

The next morning my parents phoned to check on me. They heard on the news about the ice storm in Oklahoma. I relayed my scary experience about the wreck. The first thing my dad said was, "Are you OK? You weren't hurt were you?"

"I'm fine. I was lucky no one hit me when my car spun out of control," I answered back, anticipating the next statement from him would be a lecture about my driving. Instead he responded, "Sue, ice is very hard to drive on. I'm glad you didn't get hurt. You can always replace a car. I'm sure this accident will teach you to slow down and be more careful while driving."

After that experience, I took Dad's critique of my driving skills to heart.

Love is kind. In some instances of parenting, actions speak louder than words. My dad taught me a lot about love through his acts of kindness.

He was always told when one of his children stayed home sick. Inevitably, he would come home for lunch and have a special treat in his pocket—a favorite candy bar. Receiving a candy bar was like receiving a present back in those days. I loved getting those candy bars. I had the usual childhood sicknesses: measles, mumps, and bouts with the flu, each of which brought me several of my favorite candy bars.

One day, though, I decided I needed a day off and faked an illness. That morning, I put on the sick face and complained of a sore throat and headache. Mom was very empathetic and called the school to say I would be absent.

However, the plan backfired when Dad walked through the front door at noon for lunch and caught me doing something that a sick child would not feel like doing. I was gleefully jumping up and down on the brown sectional sofa in the living room while watching *Captain Kangaroo*. Jumping on the sofa was forbidden in our household, and I knew it. However, the temptation to make the sofa a trampoline was just too overpowering.

Dad's sudden appearance brought me to a dead stop. "Well," he said, "you must be feeling much better." I tried putting on the sick routine, but I could tell from his smile he was not buying it. Instead, he made a deal with me that day. I had to return to school for the afternoon, which I did. Upon arrival from school I would then receive the candy bar.

Dad was considerate when it came to certain people and situations. A few older widows in our town depended on his helping hand. Each fall they phoned to see if he could check their furnaces and light the pilot.

I answered the phone many times throughout the years when one particularly frail woman with a polite voice would call and request to talk to Floyd. That voice belonged to Bessie Long.

I still hear the words often spoken by my dad in response to this call.

"No, I have the time, Bessie. I will be right down."

Dad was also generous with his time when it came to coaching Little League baseball. He coached the Dallas County Yankees for many years. His coaching style went hand-in-hand with his parenting style. He was a teacher with a lot of patience and kindness. He could cultivate talent in youngsters through encouragement and praise. He had many successful seasons.

I spent many evenings at the baseball field with Dad and my brothers. I was his "bat girl," and when I got older, I became his official scorekeeper.

Oh, how I loved my dad for being the coach of all those boys! I think I had a crush on a different one every week. I especially liked the away games because some of my favorite players would ride in our car. On these occasions, I had an assigned seat in the car. It was the left backseat next to the window behind his driver's seat. I'm not sure why he placed me there, but that was fine with me.

On one trip, my curiosity got the better of me. Dad always placed a brown sack behind his seat before we left. I nonchalantly opened the bag and pulled out a box that said "protector." "What is this?" I asked.

"Sue, put that back in the bag." Dad immediately responded above the laughter from the boys in the car.

But I didn't give it up. "No, I want to know what this is."

"I'll tell you later, but not right now," he sternly said.

He did explain why the catcher needed that protector during the games. He provided enough detail to satisfy my inquiring mind, and I never pulled that sack from behind his seat again.

Parenting is full of teachable moments, many of them humorous. We never know the impact our words and actions have on a child until they reach adulthood. However, I find myself applying the same advice and support my father gave in many situations with our children.

Yes, being a parent is the greatest race you will ever be assigned to run. Like any good race, you must give it lots of energy and do the best you can. The results may not be what you expected, but keep trying and never give up.

What my father taught me about parenting is this: Love is patient and love is kind. But the greatest is—love for your child.

Ninth Race:
Unexpected Losses

Running makes you an athlete in all areas of life ... trained in basics, prepared for whatever comes, ready to live each day, fill each hour and deal with the decisive moment.

George Sheehan, MD

Life is full of unexpected moments. Matthew 6:34 states, "Therefore, do not worry about tomorrow, for tomorrow will worry about itself. Each day has enough trouble of its own."

The phone call came at 3:00 PM on a dreary, cold November Monday in 1993, while I sat at my desk in the kitchen paying the monthly bills. Our three girls were asleep upstairs, and the house was peaceful. It was exactly four days since our youngest daughter, Maria, had been born. The caller ID showed my sister's number. I was eager to talk to her about Maria's birth without the kids interrupting, but she immediately blurted out, "It's back. Dad's cancer is back!"

I was silenced by the news.

"No, this can't be happening," I mumbled. My eyes welled up with tears, and my throat constricted. It was hard to breathe. Sheila relayed all the information she had about Dad's condition. "He has one of the best oncologists in Des Moines," she continued. "Chemotherapy will start in one week."

After hanging up the phone, I sat frozen at my desk, tears streaming down my face. I knew in my heart that this was not good news for Dad. He had only one lung. It had been thirteen years since his first bout with lung cancer. He had already beaten the odds of survival once.

I immediately called my mother and discussed the prognosis. Mom assured me that they had one of the best doctors in Des Moines and that his aggressive treatment plan would start soon.

I sensed alarm in my mom's voice. Even though her faith was one of the strongest I had ever witnessed, I knew she was thinking the same thing I was. We needed God's healing hand. We needed a miracle.

I asked to talk to Dad. He quickly came to the phone and asked about his newest granddaughter. I shared the details about Maria and how her two sisters were reacting to their new sibling. I couldn't avoid the subject any longer, and finally asked, "Dad, how are you feeling?"

"I'm feeling OK today. I'm just worried about the chemotherapy and the side effects."

"Dad, you'll beat this. I know you can do it. You are strong and will overcome the cancer just like you did the last time."

"I hope so," he responded.

We said our usual good-byes, and when I told him I loved him, I meant it more than ever. Sometimes we take life for granted. We think it will last forever, but life is a gift with an unknown expiration date.

After hanging up the phone, it occurred to me what Dad meant years ago. *Sue, there is always another race to run.* It was not about running a mile run any longer. It was about the races we have to run in life. And this race would be the toughest for Dad to run and the toughest for me to watch from the sidelines.

Dad was scheduled to start chemotherapy the following Monday; however, he and Mom had not met their newest granddaughter, Maria Belle. So we planned to meet for lunch on Sunday. John and I had just relocated to Kansas City from Virginia, which put us much closer to Iowa. After some discussion about a good meeting spot, we decided to meet halfway.

We met at Toot Toot's Restaurant in Bethany, Missouri. Dad suggested the restaurant for two reasons. It had a big buffet, and our family was known for enjoying large dinners with lots of food to choose from. He also thought the grandchildren would love the restaurant's railroad theme and electric trains circling the ceiling.

For some reason, the name of the restaurant struck me funny. And our daughters, Anna and Sara, and their cousins had fun connecting the name to a bodily function with sound effects. Personally, I would have named it something else like Choo Choo's. But it did give us something to joke about during lunch. It seemed to be the only thing we laughed about that day.

Dad was very quiet. I saw worry in his eyes. His usual bright smile had diminished, except when he met Maria for the first time. For a moment, he was able to hide his preoccupation with his upcoming treatment.

Dad held and fussed over her, the proud grandfather. He talked to her as though she understood him. He even noticed that she was smaller than her two sisters were at birth. Then he looked at me and said, "She has her mother's eyes."

That day was bittersweet. Maria was barely one week old, healthy and ready to begin life. My dad was only sixty-five, with cancer cells in his one remaining lung and with chemotherapy commencing in less than twenty-four hours. Without the chemo, he would most surely die.

The chemotherapy was exceptionally hard on his body. He lost weight and lost his hair. Losing the hair was a difficult thing to accept. Regardless of the change in his appearance, he was still a trooper. He kept a positive outlook and held tightly to hope. Hope that he would beat the cancer. Hope that he would win this difficult race in life.

Christmas of 1993 was a challenging time for everyone. When I arrived at my parents' house with my family on Christmas Eve, my dad was not at the door to greet us as he had every other arrival. Instead, he was seated at the kitchen table in a chair facing the front door so he could see all of us bound through the door. I was not prepared for what I saw. I was stunned by his appearance. He was pale, thinner, and appeared weak. The chemotherapy the past few weeks had taken a heavy toll on his body.

Nevertheless, he tremulously rose like a gentleman to give me a hug and greet his granddaughters and John. Even though he was ill, he still radiated love and compassion.

My brothers and sister and their families were present this Christmas as well. Dad even appeared to have an inexplicable spike of energy on Christmas Day. Many pictures were taken, and the video camera rolled continuously. There was a lot of love, laughter, and, of course, food shared in the home where I grew up—a home filled with wonderful memories that would be imprinted in my mind forever. Time seemed to stop for all of us on that day.

Dad seemed to rebound by spring of 1994. The cancer had not metastasized and he stopped the chemotherapy. I decided to take a week in March and go visit my parents. John could not go because of his work schedule. Mom was excited to hear that the girls and I were coming home. She said, "It will lift your dad's spirits to have you and the kids here."

One day during my stay, I asked Dad if he would like to take a car ride. When I was a child and Dad suggested taking a ride, it meant fun and adventure. We never knew where he would drive us, but many times it would turn out that the ride had its own purpose.

Today's ride had such a purpose. Even though I was the one to suggest the ride, Dad wanted to drive. I was glad to turn over the wheel. I recognized his desire to drive as a sign that it was a good day for him.

It was a beautiful day with a hint of spring in the air. The sun shone brightly, and its warmth was almost tangible. The grass was starting to sprout in yards, and the hillsides in the country looked like a fresh, green carpet.

Dad drove me around to a few houses he had liked when he was working as a serviceman for Iowa Power and Light. He would point out the big beautiful homes and tell me a little bit about each family. I was intrigued that he took such an interest in these people and could recall such details about their lives.

The highlight of the ride was when he drove me by some homes he had tried to persuade my mother to buy. We both laughed at the chance of Mom ever moving from her first and only home. Dad said she thought each home was very nice, but she found a few things wrong with all of them, and therefore they had never moved.

My parents bought their first home in 1953. It was a simple white frame house with a wraparound porch. It had one of each—bedroom, dining room, living room, bathroom, and kitchen. When my second brother, Randy, was born, Dad's coworker, Punch Merical, helped open up the attic and add two new bedrooms. More remodeling followed over the years to transform the home to accommodate the needs of our growing family.

My mother's pride and joy was the kitchen. She worked closely with the remodeling contractor to design the perfect kitchen with her family dinners in mind. Never a holiday went by without some of our relatives seated around the table.

My parents especially made sure that not a single one of our elderly relatives spent the holidays alone.

I told Dad that day that Mom loved her house because of all the happy memories generated inside those walls. I then recalled the many holiday meals served from her kitchen. "You know Mom. She has never been impressed by the 'bigger is better' mentality," I said with a grin on my face. Dad smiled and nodded in agreement.

During this car ride, I had the opportunity to ask my dad some questions about a time in his life I'd been curious about. I had been particularly fascinated about the time he played semi-professional baseball for the New York Yankees. Although Dad had enjoyed this opportunity, he never really talked too much about it.

Today, he told stories about seeing the ocean for the first time and meeting some good ball players. At that point, I asked one of my questions.

"Dad, how good of a pitcher were you?"

"I wasn't bad," he responded.

"Were you faster than Denny or Randy?"

"Maybe a little faster." He grinned.

That's one of the many things I loved about my father—his humility. I suspect my dad was really fast and really good, but he would never admit it. Another life lesson he taught me growing up. *Let other people brag about you, but don't brag about yourself.*

The next question on my mind had to do with baseball, too. "Dad, do you have regrets about giving up your dream of playing in the big leagues?"

"No, Sue, I really don't. If I had continued to play and made it to the major leagues, I would have never met your mother and had you kids."

His answer left me speechless for a few moments. I turned my head away from him and gazed out the window. I didn't want him to see my tears. I thought to myself, *His family means so much to him.*

Then I felt the urge to speak.

"Dad, you have been the best father to me and husband to Mom that anyone could ever ask for."

"Thank you, Sue. I've tried to be."

The car ride ended shortly after that conversation. I didn't have any more questions. My dad's comments will be with me forever.

On Easter Sunday of 1994, Dad and I attended church together. The walk up the stairs of the First Christian Church winded him. It worried me, but once inside, he perked up. Many church members came over and greeted him. Even the pastor made a point to say hello. Dad thought very highly of this pastor and his church.

My parents were married in this church in 1950 and had been active members ever since. They were committed to serving God. They had the same expectations for their children. We were expected to attend Sunday school and worship every

Sunday, unless we were sick. Church services were always hard for me to sit through as a child.

My parents sat strategically with their four children during the services. We were placed on each side of them. I sat next to my dad as often as possible, because when I got restless, he would reach inside his suit coat pocket and pull out a piece of Wrigley's Juicy Fruit or spearmint gum. Occasionally, he would have one of those red-and-white peppermint candies tucked away, too. Those treats usually settled me down, except for one Sunday when my brother Randy decided to imitate a woman singing in the choir.

It was one of those situations where you know you must be silent out of respect for the preacher and God, but you can't contain your laughter for the life of you. I tried really hard to hold the giggles inside. But when my body started to shake and bounce up and down on the pew, the inevitable happened. An outburst of laughter shot out of me like a cannon.

It goes down as being another one of my embarrassing moments in life. The pastor paused, my dad cupped his hand over my mouth, and my mom looked mortified. Needless to say, I received a major scolding from Mom on the way home from church that day. However, Dad spoke up in agreement with me. "That woman opened her mouth so wide today that you could drive a train through it." Mom didn't think that was very funny, but I did.

This Easter Sunday as I sat silently, while a flood of memories flowed through my mind about time spent in this church as a child with my family, especially with Dad.

Dad was well respected in our church. He served on the board as an elder and a deacon. He enjoyed being a deacon best. He loved serving communion and helping those in need in our congregation. Dad had a quiet faith and a servant's heart.

He once told me that he didn't like being an elder as well because you have to get up in front of the congregation and speak. Speaking in front of people made Dad nervous. When he had to speak, I would pray doubly hard to God for help. I believe God heard my prayers. Dad did just fine. I often told him that. One time he said, "Sometimes we just have to make ourselves do things we don't want to do."

Since Dad's most recent diagnosis, I had tried to see him as often as possible. Father's Day was the next major holiday. However, this year the day took on a different meaning. In the back of my mind I wondered if this would be his last, or if there would be many more to come. No one can predict the future. Only God knows what lies ahead for each person.

Although Dad seemed to be doing well, he looked thinner than usual. His beautiful gray hair had grown back with its natural curl. I often remind my oldest daughter, Sara, that she has Grandpa's curls. Many family pictures were taken of Dad with me and my girls on this weekend. And as always, Dad would stand proudly over his granddaughters and daughter and smile with love.

In August we planned a family weekend at the Lake of the Ozarks in Laurie, Missouri, where my parents had a vacation home. Dad delighted in having his children and grandchildren at the lake. Of course, Mom delighted in her family, too, but focused more on planning and cooking all the food for the gathering.

Dad was proud of his twenty-foot speedboat. He should have been. He had worked hard all his life and deserved to have a few luxuries. His greatest joy came not from ownership, however, but from letting his children water-ski, towing the grandchildren in an inflatable raft, or taking everyone for a boat ride.

During one particular trip, he announced he had a surprise for the grandchildren. He told all of us to hop into the boat. We were going to lunch. Everyone did as instructed and headed out on the lake for the mystery ride. The adventurous boat ride lasted for several miles before coming to rest in front of a restaurant named "Frogs."

Dad chose this restaurant for the grandchildren. The interior of the restaurant had a frog theme, which immediately grabbed the children's attention. He was right; the grandchildren loved looking at all the frog paraphernalia, and the adults enjoyed a peaceful meal.

On the boat ride back, Dad asked for any takers on water-skiing. No one readily volunteered, so Dad volunteered me. He excitedly said, "Sue, show your girls how you can water-ski!" I decided to take the challenge. Jokingly, I said, "I hope I can still get up out of the water."

I slipped off my bathing-suit pullover, buckled up the life jacket, and plunged into the water. After I got situated behind the boat with my skis perpendicular and clutching the tow rope, I told Dad I was ready with the classic cue: "Hit it!" He gunned the boat, and I popped right out of the water and skied all the way to the lake home. Dad turned slightly so I could see his big smile and his victory wave—the famous gestures I had witnessed so many times over the years.

Dad seemed much stronger and happier that weekend. I had a surge of hope that he was going to beat the cancer. I started to believe that God was performing a miracle.

As Labor Day approached, I had a strong feeling that I needed to make a visit to see Dad. I went, taking only our youngest daughter with me. When I arrived home, Dad was using an oxygen tank at bedtime, but was still ambulatory and able to talk. He appeared much weaker than ever before. *How could this be? How could this happen so quickly?* It was heart wrenching to see him struggling like this.

I planned to leave Monday afternoon and return to Kansas City. I sensed Mom needed a break to run some errands, so Monday morning, I suggested she take some time to go shopping. I assured her that Dad, Maria, and I would be fine without her for a few hours.

After putting Maria down for a nap, I found Dad sitting in the family room, staring out the sliding glass windows at some birds. Dad loved watching and feeding birds. His favorite bird was the male cardinal. I agree—the bright red male cardinal is, in my opinion, the most beautiful bird God ever created.

I felt I needed to use this time to tell him some things in my heart. But I didn't want him to think I was saying this because it might be our last conversation.

I was very concerned about Dad's breathing patterns. I suggested that I give him a back rub. He seemed to appreciate that little gesture. I pulled a chair up beside his chair and rubbed his shoulders in the hope that I could make his breathing better. I made sure I was positioned behind him so he couldn't see the panic in my eyes. Dad could always pick up on my emotions no matter how hard I tried to hide them.

"Dad, for some time I've wanted to thank you for being such a great dad. You were always there for me. Especially at all those track meets. And you never missed a mile run. And when I wanted to quit track, you wouldn't let me. I'm so thankful for that, Dad."

I couldn't continue because I felt a knot form in my throat and tears begin to well up in my eyes. There was so much more I needed to say, but I could not force the words out of my mouth.

"Sue, you were a good runner. No one can be first all the time. You know, sometimes you learn more from your losses."

I still couldn't speak, so he continued.

"Enjoy your life and your children. Life on earth goes by so quickly. People used to tell me that all the time when I was younger, but I really didn't think about time running out."

"You are the best dad that anyone could ever ask for."

Instead of Dad taking the compliment, he responded in his usual humble way.

He smiled gently. "You know, your mother is the best mother anyone could ask for. She is so proud of her children, and oh, how she loves those grandchildren."

"I know, Dad, how good Mom is and how she loves us all," I responded.

There was still more to say, but his comment about my mom choked me up even more. I thought, *here is a man struggling with cancer, unable to breathe without oxygen at times, but he's still talking about my mother in such a loving way.* He taught me something very important that afternoon. *That one of the greatest gifts we have to give is love for one another.*

I left that afternoon to return to Kansas City. I cried off and on during the four-hour drive. I had the feeling that God was trying to prepare me for the inevitable.

When I was a child, my mom had taught me to say my prayers on my knees beside my bed. I prayed that way until my high-school years. However, this particular Monday night, I needed to be on my knees praying like I'd never prayed before.

I couldn't stand watching my dad struggle for life any longer. I sobbed out loud this prayer: "Please, God, don't let him suffer anymore. He is a good man and has been a wonderful dad. He never hurt anyone in his life. I can't watch my dad suffer like this. Please, God, help him. Amen."

One week later I received a phone call around 6:30 AM from my brother Randy. Before I answered, I knew it would not be good news. Dad had been hospitalized shortly after my visit.

"Sue, you need to come home today. Mom just called from the hospital; Dad is not doing well. Dr. Temple told her to call her children."

"I will try to get there by this afternoon. I can't believe this is happening so fast."

"Hurry, Sue. I don't think Dad is going to make it through the day."

"I'll get there as fast as I can, but please tell Dad that I love him," I said as I hung up the phone.

After making arrangements for someone to watch the girls, I was speeding north on Interstate 35 by 9:00 AM. I rode in silence, except for the times I talked to God. I asked him to keep Dad alive long enough so I could see him one more time.

It was 12:20 when I pulled my white minivan into the parking lot of Iowa Methodist Medical Center. I grabbed my purse and slipped off my sandals, and the moment my feet hit the pavement, I ran toward the hospital like I had never run before. I ran until I found the elevators that took me to the third floor.

As I entered his room, Dad looked up and barely smiled.

"They are all here now."

Dad slipped into a coma shortly after I arrived. The morphine drip was increased to keep him comfortable and help with his pain. I held his hand in silence. At approximately 4:20 PM that day, September 13, 1994, my beloved dad died. He was sixty-six years old.

There is no way to accurately describe your feelings on the day of your father's death—especially a relationship like ours. It is a surreal experience with a feeling of numbness. Death ended his life, but not our relationship. It is a day I will never forget.

I guess you could say cancer was declared the winner on this day. But Dad fought it with perseverance, dignity, and grace. He ran the race the best he could.

Tenth Race: Reflection on a Great Run

In the long run, we shape our lives and we shape ourselves. The process never ends until we die, and the choices that we make are ultimately our responsibility.

Eleanor Roosevelt

The funeral was held at the First Christian Church in Adel, three days after Dad's death, the same church where in the past, joyous family occasions had taken place: my parents' marriage, the baptisms of four children, four grandchildren's baby dedications, and my oldest brother's wedding.

This September day turned out to be a sunny, crisp, fall day. You are always thankful for the sunshine on such a sorrow-filled day. The day seemed to be ordered especially for Dad.

Timothy Johnson (Pastor Tim as we called him) conducted the funeral. Dad thought the world of his pastor. Tim was known for preaching strong sermons, and on this day, he again proved himself. He performed a funeral that was a tribute to my dad for the way he lived his life and the choices that he made.

Pastor Tim compared the Golden Rule to how Dad lived his life: "*Do unto others what you would have them do unto you.* I suppose we think it is 'golden' because it defines such a wonderful ideal. In many ways, Floyd practiced that rule." Then he added, "I don't know how you think of God, especially in times when you're thinking about the death of someone who still had a lot of living to do, but Jesus makes an interesting comparison. God is like a father. God thinks of us as a loving father thinks of his children. I think Floyd's the kind of father Jesus had in mind when he made that comparison.

"Floyd loved his kids and his grandchildren with a pride and a love that was deeply ingrained in him. He loved them in a manner that allowed his love to be obvious in his eyes and in his expression when he was near his kids or they were the topic of conversation.

"Floyd's children remember that he was always at all of their school events, and that required effort and scheduling on Floyd's part to make it happen. They remember he was there to watch and help out. For instance, he thoroughly enjoyed being a time keeper at track meets. His daughter, Sue, remembers that she'd watch for Floyd's truck to pull in, for she could expect him to make it in time to see her run. She recalls the way he'd stand by the track and call out her split times as she ran her mile.

"Whether it was a winning day or a losing day, Floyd was there for his kids. Watching, cheering, coaching Little

League—letting his sons and daughters know that they were important, that they were loved by their father."

This comment brought a smile to my face and more tears to my eyes. Yes, my dad was always there for me. He never missed a mile run—never. He was always there to watch me run that race.

Tim mentioned Dad's pitching opportunity for the New York Yankees farm club system. My father was a very humble man, and so many people, including his own children, didn't realize how good he had been at America's favorite pastime.

Tim continued, "He was drafted by the New York Yankees right out of high school, and for over two years, he pitched for them. That's pretty impressive, but it is even more impressive when you read the article that told of Floyd's record that got the scouts' attention. He went 21-8 in two seasons—that's a terrific win/loss record. He pitched five shut-outs and one no-hitter. In 199 innings he struck out 299 batters." I learned something that day even if Dad would not admit it. He had been a powerful pitcher.

Pastor Tim went on to relay other important events from my dad's life and the impact he had made. My father was also described as a good and loving husband.

Then, Pastor Tim challenged all who attended this funeral service. "Do you remember the scripture we started with? It talked about being a good father and about treating other people in the manner you would like to be treated. Well, Floyd Seibert lived like that. Whether it was the August vacations he made a priority to take with his family or the way he tried to take care of people with respect and generosity; this man reflected the idea the scriptures talk about. When we pause because someone we care about has died, it's a good time for us to look at our relationship with God. Here's a thought for you: When you fully trust in God, you know that God's love will never fail you. Nothing can separate you from God's love. Circumstances may sometimes cause you to feel forsaken, but you never are. You may temporarily fail to enjoy the presence and love of God because of your hurts or fears. But God's love is still there. Circumstances don't change the reality of God's presence and love—even though you may change in your awareness of them. God remains lovingly faithful and faithfully loving. God doesn't change."

Pastor Tim concluded by saying, "The promises and the memories of Floyd's life are the reason we celebrate today. His kids remember that Floyd taught them to work hard and to do their best. He taught them never to give up and that it didn't matter how you placed as long as you finished. Floyd's family holds a glorious memory, for they know that they came first with Floyd, and the result is a familial closeness and love that will help them through all that life throws their way.

"Please think of the promises your Creator offers you. You might know these words from John 3:16, 'For God so loved the world, that He gave His one and only Son, that whoever believes in Him shall not perish, but have eternal life.'

"I imagine that Floyd has heard his God welcome him into heaven, for he believed. Maybe God's words to him will reflect Matthew 25:23, 'Well done, good and faithful servant! You have been faithful over a few things; I will put you in charge of many things. Come and share your master's happiness!'"

The concluding prayer is worth sharing. It went like this:

Dear God, we pause now to thank you for the life of Floyd Henry Seibert. For the good he did and for the love he shared, we are eternally thankful. For the manner in which he cared for his family, we are grateful for the example.

Please give him welcome and mercy, love and peace as you welcome him into the next part of his living, and reassure him of the love his people hold for him in this place. Bless Ruby and Floyd's sons, daughters, and grandchildren with a sense of his love always.

Now we give thanks to you for our days. Might we love well and treat one another in the right way. Might we work well and might we add our best to the world around us. All of this as Floyd did, leaving the world a better place for his years.

Thank you for this day and for the life of this man. Amen.

During the car ride to the cemetery for Dad's burial, I pondered life. One day you are on earth, and then on one specific, chosen day, you die. On this day, I wanted time to stop. In fact, I wanted every car we passed to pull over in respect for my dad's life. That was something he had taught me to do for a funeral processional. And most important, I wanted the passers-by to know that a good man had died and left a legacy of love.

As Abraham Lincoln said, "And in the end it's not the years in your life that count. It's the life in your years."

Reflecting on my father's overall life, I would say—he had a great run! He, like anyone, had triumphs, trials and struggles. He was not perfect, no one is. But I think if he could answer the question Was life worth running the race?, his response definitely would be—yes!

Eleventh Race: Overcoming Obstacles

Success is to be measured not so much by the position that one has reached in life as by the obstacles which he has overcome while trying to succeed.

Booker T. Washington

Grief is a tough race to run. It is filled with many obstacles.

Dad taught me so much about living life. What he didn't teach me was how to live life without him. Or maybe he had.

"The more we love, the deeper we grieve," the pastor said in his Sunday morning sermon. Those words penetrated my soul more than anyone will ever know. My grief felt like an earthquake that shook me to the core.

The first few weeks following Dad's death, I stumbled around in a state of denial.

The reality finally set in when I called home for the first time, and Dad did not answer the phone. Dad was typically the one who answered the phone and would chat for a few minutes so he could catch up on all the latest about his grand-daughters, my activities, and John's job. He was also always curious about the weather where we were living. When our usual routine of chatting was over, he would say, "There's someone standing right next to me who can't wait to talk to you." Then he would hand the phone to my mom.

There were many "firsts" the year after Dad's death. Thanksgiving dinner without him helping in the kitchen or presiding at the head of the table produced a somber mood among all of us.

Christmas was especially hard on me. Dad always enjoyed shopping for his children and his wife. And he delighted in finding the perfect gifts for his grandchildren, too. It was apparent which ones he specifically selected for them in the way he watched with great intent and looked victorious when they opened their gifts and squealed with excitement.

Then with great pride, he would hand each of his children an envelope with a money gift tucked inside. Dad enjoyed giving to others. He not only taught me that it is better to give than to receive, but to give with your heart, soul, and a big smile!

Something else was missing that Christmas Day—Dad's sense of humor. He was notorious for shaking each one of his gifts and then guessing what was inside before unwrapping it. He would even thank the giver ahead of time. And he nailed what was inside the package every time. Each year he thanked someone for his Old Spice cologne, a new wallet, sweater, or a tool.

One year I tricked him though. I had purchased a life preserver that had "The Seiberts" printed on it. I thought the preserver would look great hanging by the back door of their lake home to welcome guests.

I wrapped it in a large box and stuffed it with lots of newspaper. For the life of him, he could not guess the contents of this package. He even tried coercing me into giving him some hints, but my lips remained sealed. When he finally opened the gift, his expression revealed his astonishment and excitement. He loved it. He also knew exactly what it was for and announced where he would hang it.

I decided that January 1 would be a good day to start running again on a consistent schedule. I needed to run for so many reasons. I needed it to help me with the grief I was experiencing. I needed it to release stress so I could cope with raising our three darling daughters. And I needed it to help me shed a few pounds from having my third child.

Running took on a different meaning for me. I thought a lot about my dad while I ran and would play his words in my mind often. *Don't give up, keep going, Sue. Do your best. There's always another race to run.*

There was a tape I played often in my Sony walkman during the morning runs. My favorite song became "Because You Loved Me" by Celine Dion. The lyrics reminded me of all the support Dad had given me over the years. The words ministered to my soul and gave me extra energy for my morning run, especially up the hill toward the end of the course.

Dad would have been sixty-seven on February 21, another day on the calendar that was tough to endure. My thoughts were about him throughout this special day. I wished our family was all together, eating with him at his favorite restaurant.

It was a week before Easter, and I was having a tough time. That is the way grief works sometimes. The tears appear unannounced. One morning, I was standing at the kitchen sink washing dishes with my head hung low as tears streamed down my face. I started talking out loud to God.

"I miss him so much. I just wish he was still here," I cried.

At that moment God silently whispered to my broken heart. *Look up, Sue, and listen.*

I immediately recognized something special in the pine tree. A bright red cardinal was perched there, singing his heart out and looking straight at me. I stared at him for the longest time. When he eventually hopped from the branch and flew away, I looked toward heaven and said, "Thank you." From that day forward, every time I see a cardinal, I look up and say, *Thank you, God.*

Father's Day was one of the darkest days I ever experienced. The emotions hit me like a torrent. Going to church was out of the question. I couldn't bear to hear a sermon or prayer about fathers. I wept intermittently all day long. I stayed in my home and occasionally peered out the window at the red sunset maple that I had planted in the front yard the week before in honor of my dad. The maple tree would give me a sense of comfort in years to come, no matter where I lived.

This gesture may seem strange to some; however, I even purchased a card for him one day while browsing through a store. I was faithful about buying the perfect card each year to tell Dad how important he was to me. I wished I could have mailed this one to him in heaven. Even though there were so many things I wished I'd said, I felt this card summed it up well. It simply expressed the love and appreciation I had for him.

Many years have passed since I bought that card. However, the loving memories my father left behind will stay with me forever. Memories do last forever. It's something no one can take away from you.

The first anniversary of Dad's death on September 13, 1995, was still very vivid. It felt like a play in which I had memorized my script perfectly. I relived every hour as if it were the actual day he died. The past year had me going through the motions of life for many events and not really feeling anything. However, this day I felt the real pain, and I didn't like it. I wanted something or someone to take the pain away. And I longed to have my dad back living on this earth. But I realized that would never be possible.

My mom and I talked almost daily after Dad's death that first year. She had lost the man she loved and adored for forty-four years. She missed him terribly, but involved herself with church work, friends and the grandchildren. She visited us often and we spent many hours talking about the memories of him. She was strong and relied on her faith to help her deal with her loss.

John had a hard time understanding why I could not snap out of the grief quicker. He had not lost a parent and therefore could not comprehend my emotions. At times, I felt alone and that no one understood me. It put a strain on our marriage, which had already shown some signs of weakness earlier. My faith was tested, too. I questioned God—Why did Dad have to die? In hindsight, I wish I had joined a grief support group or talked to a pastor.

The grieving period is different for everyone. The first year was tough, but by the second year, the emotional roller coaster of feelings and emotions leveled off. I still had private moments when I would think of him and tears would well up. I don't think that ever goes away. However, I began to feel like my old self again. And I began enjoying life again—just like Dad had advised me to do one week before he died.

However, life took on a different meaning for me. I valued life much more and appreciated every God-given day granted to me on this earth. I also reexamined my purpose in life. The experts say if you work through your grief and don't get stuck, much growth will occur. So grief will produce growth. To grow, you must try new things.

I began to play the piano. I had taken piano lessons when I was a child for a couple of years but did not stick with it. In fact, it was my dad who made me make a decision about my continuation of piano lessons.

I remember how one day he happened to walk into the room as I was practicing on the white piano that my mom had purchased through the classifieds of the Dallas County News.

Dad was grinning with his arms crossed over his chest when he delivered this message to me.

"Sue, you can really pound out that piece of music quite well, but that seems to be the only piece I ever hear you practice. I've noticed on the classical songs, Mrs. Beal has you repeat the lesson week after week. I can't continue to pay for lessons when all you ever play is "Proud Mary." You need to make a decision. Do you want to continue taking piano lessons and try different songs or play sports?" It wasn't a hard decision for me. I didn't like practicing the piano at all and my desire was always toward sports.

"I want to play sports." And that was the end of my piano lessons for that period of my life.

Now, at thirty-six years old, I decided to take piano lessons.

My goal in taking lessons was to learn to play again, especially Christmas carols. When I mastered the carols and a few other songs, my piano teacher asked me if there was a particular song I would like to play. I grinned and said, "Yes! 'Proud Mary' by Creedence Clearwater Revival!"

To this day, I can still pound out that song. I would bet that my dad is looking down from heaven thinking—*maybe all that money spent on piano lessons was not a total waste.*

Winston Churchill said, "We make a living by what we get, but we make a life by what we give."

My father gave so much to others in need that it became my pursuit to emulate this after his death. I realized it was important for our girls to see me helping other people just like Dad had.

My passion for helping people centered on children, the poor, and the elderly. Those were the three areas where I had witnessed Dad volunteering. In fact, after his death we received a note with a return address from Adel Acres Nursing Center. It was from Bessie Long, who was in her early nineties at the time. She wrote a touching note about Dad's many acts of kindness. He was remembered by many for his selfless nature.

The sunset red maple tree I planted in my front yard became a gentle reminder of Dad's goodness. After many of my morning runs I would finish by standing in front of the tree. Often, I would talk out loud to the tree as if I were having a conversation with Dad. I would always take hold of a branch as if it were my dad's hand. He always had that consoling hand, and somehow this simple tree gave me comfort and support amidst my grief.

The tree was symbolic of all the races I had run. It reminded me of the tree where Dad stood. He was always there with his words of encouragement to keep running the race.

Little did I know what the future held for me—for the next race to run was going to be the most painful event in my life.

Twelfth Race:
The Humongous Hill

Bid me run and I will strive with things impossible.

William Shakespeare

I once commented to Marguerite, my eighty-five-year-old friend that I wished I knew what the future held for me. Her response startled me. "No, you don't, Sue. If you knew, it would scare you." It wasn't long after her comment that I realized what she was implying.

I thought my dad's death was a painful experience. However, the next major life experience for me was worse than death.

I have learned one thing about life. It can be hard. No one gets through it without some pain and suffering. The unknown will occur at different times in your life. And it may be presented in different forms of physical, mental, or emotional affliction. Sometimes things happen that you may never understand, but you stride ahead, hoping to make it through the race.

Around the eighteenth year of my marriage problems erupted. The timing could not have been worse. It occurred during a transition in life—a major career move for John to Cincinnati, Ohio, from Kansas City. This relocation in June of 2000 took us far away from family, friends, and my church. Before this move we were having some marital troubles. I had opened up an email that was sent to an address we both shared. It was obvious the message wasn't intended for me. But after we moved I had more time to think and question John about the situation. He finally admitted to infidelity.

I felt like someone had taken a sledge hammer and slugged me full force in the stomach. This devastating blow threw my mind, body, and soul into an almost catatonic state. I was like a robot going through the motions while feeling very little. It was almost what I would imagine an out-of-body experience feels like.

My first reaction was to run. Run away from life. So I did. I traveled with the children for a week to a place that provided shelter for my searching soul—the beautiful beaches of Corolla, North Carolina. It was a perfect island setting to ponder life.

I had discovered Corolla while living in Virginia Beach from 1989 to 1993. This charming seaside village is located in the northern part of the Outer Banks. I fell in love immediately with the towering pine trees, gorgeous sunsets, and alluring Atlantic Ocean.

During this stay, we toured the Currituck Lighthouse. After climbing 214 stairs, we reached the top where the view was magnificent for miles. This particular day, the ocean was raging with white-capped waves. It reflected the emotional and mental turmoil within me. The other side of the lighthouse presented a totally different scene. The Currituck Sound side was serene—a feeling my soul longed for.

However, it would be some time before I felt that calmness return. The getaway was refreshing, but it did not solve my marital problems. They were still waiting for me when we returned home. John and I tried working things out over the next year by seeking marital counseling as we had done in the past to deal with our issues.

As a result of my distraught state of mind, I did some crazy things. On several occasions, I spent money like it really did grow on trees. Like, for example, the time when one daughter wanted a bunk bed, and I decided to purchase three to make everyone happy. I got even more generous when the men delivered those beds. I gave one man a nearly new trundle bed for his child and a fifty-dollar tip so they could buy lunch. Their surprised smiles told me I had made their day.

I also spent way too much money on clothing and jewelry in just a few months. When I eyed a top or slacks I liked, I ordered it in every color. I finally came to my senses when I started receiving bills for my impulsive buys. Luckily, the return policies were still in effect, and I was able to return approximately ninety percent of the items. The shopping sprees stopped.

However, there was one action I will always regret. Upon moving into the new house in Ohio, I had many boxes to unpack. One day, I discovered my trophies and medals from track and cross country. Instead of just resealing the box, I hauled them out to the curb for the trash pickup. At one point in my life, I was very proud of this box of accomplishments. However, on this day, I was upset about my marital problems and could care less about the happiness this box of stuff brought me at one time. Nothing really mattered anymore except for one thing—the children.

I knew I had to keep it together for the girls who were now six, eight, and eleven. I was determined not to let life break me. But you can only hide the pain behind a smile for so long. Eventually the sadness showed. For awhile, they just thought I hated living in Ohio. However, it didn't take them long to sense something was very wrong between their parents. Maria asked a question one day that left me speechless. "Why don't you kiss Daddy anymore?"

The darkest days of my life were ahead. I felt depressed and afraid of the future most of the time. I developed stomach problems. I had many sleepless nights. And I cried a lot. But even still, I pushed myself. I tried to do something with the girls every day. During this difficult period, I also made sure I attended church every Sunday. It gave me some solace and strength to go on. One Sunday in his sermon, a Presbyterian pastor said that his parents were both dead, but he felt their presence more than ever in his life. That's exactly how I felt—that Dad's presence was right alongside me at this painful point in my life.

This was a race I did not want to run. I would have rather stayed in bed curled up like a cat with the covers over my head, but I didn't. Instead, I ran. Running became one of the most important saving graces in my life.

It was as if Dad's words of encouragement echoed down from heaven to my fragile state of mind. *Come on, Sue, get up and run. Put your right foot in front of your left and breathe. Come on ... I am not going to let you quit. You have to keep running.*

I played these words of encouragement in my mind every morning as I set out on my daily run. The route I chose reminded me of the golf course in Urbandale, Iowa, where my dad had coached me up the humongous hill at the end of the course. My life now looked like that long, steep hill—nearly impossible to ascend. But I had to keep running. Many times I pretended Dad was right there, saying, *come on, keep going, lean into the hill, breathe, you can't quit now.* And when I told myself, *I can't do this*; I heard another echo from heaven: *Yes you can.*

I ran this same course for over a year. Listening to music while I ran was good for my soul. So was reciting Psalm 23. Sometimes all I could murmur was, "The Lord is my shepherd." And when I ended in front of my new house, I would stop and touch the branch of the latest sunset maple that I had planted, once again in honor of Dad.

The running and music helped me deal with my roller-coaster feelings of anger and sadness. However, the emotions soon caught up with me. The counselor had warned me that I could not keep ignoring the reality of my situation and pretending everything was OK to the outside world. He was right. The time finally came when I had to make some decisions about my life.

The turning point occurred on a stormy Friday night in February 2001, when my emotional status matched the weather report. The thunderstorm was so strong that evening that people were cautioned not to drive because of the strong winds and rising water in many of the rivers.

My husband had phoned to say he was late leaving a business meeting. I had been anxious all day and that call did not help. In addition, I was angry that my life had taken an unexpected turn over which I had no control. I was mad at God, too, for letting this happen to me.

The minute John arrived and stepped inside the front door, I was exiting out the back. I needed to be outside—away from everyone—regardless of the weather warnings.

I didn't think I could go on anymore. There were too many decisions racing around in my mind regarding our children and my own life. And I did not feel strong enough mentally or emotionally to deal with the situation. So I drove with nowhere to go.

The road was very hilly with sharp hairpin turns. The gusty winds and sheets of rain made it difficult to drive at times. The visibility was poor due to heavy rain and my own flood of tears.

The next event changed my life forever. It was as if someone took control of the wheel and guided my car safely into a parking lot down by the river. The parking lot belonged to a church.

I got out of my car sobbing and stood under the tree and begged God to send lightning. Dad had always warned me never to stand under a tree when there was a storm—especially if there was lightning. *Because lightning likes to strike trees,* he reasoned. At that moment, I didn't care. And when God didn't respond to my request, I yelled, "Why are you doing this to me? What have I done to deserve this pain?"

Then God sent a bolt of understanding to my troubled mind. The words silently spoke to my shattered heart … *I did not do this to you, your husband did.*

I stood for a few moments speechless in front of that towering tree with lightning striking and flashing all around. Then, I finally understood. I quit blaming John and God for my troubles and realized some decisions must be made. I also thought about places I had failed in the marriage. I got in my car and drove home in a solemn state.

Before going to bed, I prayed on my knees for God to help me with my decisions of separating and where to live. I also thanked Him for not letting go of me during this turbulent storm of life. Then I crawled into bed and fell asleep with the white Bible that I had received from fourth-grade Sunday school promotion cradled in my arms.

The next morning, I announced to John that I would be moving back to Kansas City after the girls finished the school year. He said, "I take full responsibility for this, but I wish you wouldn't." I was working toward forgiveness, but I couldn't get over the betrayal. The next day, I placed a call to a realtor friend and asked him to start looking for a house for the girls and me.

The following Monday morning was full of sunshine. I was driving Sara to school when I passed the white frame church tucked beside the river where I spent Friday night in the depths of despair crying out to the omnipotent God. I noticed the marquee. It read: *God will take care of you!*

I sensed it was a reassuring message from my Heavenly Father. I recognized, too, that I had to trust Him with my life from this day forward. I held on tightly to my faith and a scripture that I had heard many times from Proverbs 3:5–6: "Trust in the Lord with all your heart and not on your own understanding; in all your ways acknowledge Him, and He will make your paths straight." My faith gave me hope—hope that everything eventually would be OK.

After I started making decisions, I called my dear friend, Susan Ashby, whom I had met while living in Virginia Beach from 1989 to 1993. I needed to tell her what was going on in my life. I was dealing with a lot of fear and anxiety and needed some reassurance. She is the person who always said the right thing at the right time. She offered this advice; "Sue, just live one day at a time. That's all you can focus on right now." That became another saving grace: *live one day at a time.* It reminded me of Dad's advice when he said, "Sue, just run the race."

Separation was inevitable although very amicable. John and I wanted to protect our children as much as possible from this horrific life change. And I always affirmed that John was a good dad. The girls and I returned to Kansas City the following summer. We also brought with us three new additions—during one of my generous moods, I let them talk me into two cats and a dog, so Daisy, our English setter, and cats Jewels and Muffin, made the trip, too.

The move went as planned, just like I trusted it would. However, I will never forget my daughter's face as we pulled away from the home we thought was going to be permanent. Our oldest daughter's expression will be stamped in my memory forever. She rode in the minivan with me and the pets. (The other two followed behind in my mother's car.) Sara's face looked defeated. *What went wrong with our family? Why didn't I see it coming?* The same questions I had pondered a million times that ran over and over in my mind. To so many people who have asked me what went wrong and wanted to know the details, my response has always been, "Sometimes things happen in life that you will never understand."

Life is a journey, and sometimes it will take a turn on the track that no one can expect. But you must keep going by putting one foot in front of the other, breathing, and moving forward. The pace you set for this race doesn't matter. What matters is that you keep going and you don't quit.

I believe that things happen for a reason. We may never fully understand the reasons, but we must hold tightly to things that are important. The things that I had been taught to hang on to were faith, family, friends, and my running. That is what got me through the devastation of a divorce.

Victory Lap:
Still Running

Life is a positive-sum game. Everyone from the gold medalist to the last finisher can rejoice in a personal victory.

George Sheehan, MD

As we run through life, we realize it is just like my dad said so many years ago: "There will always be another race to run!" He was right. Life presents many races to run. They will be mixed with victories, losses, struggles, and disappointments. We will get bumped, bruised, and scarred along the way. We may even fall down. Regardless, we must run the race set before us the best we can, and never give up. Crossing the finish line is always the goal, no matter what place we end up. That is where the victory lies.

I often think about Dad and the legacy he left. Sure, he introduced me to running, but it went far beyond the track.

He taught me a lot about living from the way he lived his life. He appreciated his life. He was a man with his priorities straight, who took his commitment to his family seriously. And by his coaching, through my races of life on and off the track, he left the greatest legacy of all: the legacy of life lessons.

His love for me was evident early on because of his genuine interest and involvement in my life. Through his love he created invaluable and sustaining memories for me. He lives on in my heart forever. Something no one can minimize or take away.

Dads teach daughters a lot from being involved in their lives. It is about taking the time to know your child and her talents. The next step is cultivating those abilities. Some children are gifted to be great. My athletic abilities were developed into being good. Yes, I loved running and still do. In fact, during the difficult divorce period, I decided to sign up for the Jared Coones Pumpkin Run. It was a local race started to honor a little boy who had died of leukemia. The course was fun, and I was proud of my finishing time, but had to leave before the awards ceremony and therefore didn't know the final results. After church the following Sunday, Pastor Bob, who had participated in the run, offered me a vigorous handshake to congratulate me on my time. He excitedly said, "Sue, did you know you placed second in your age division?" I just grinned and replied, "That's the story of my life."

Even though Dad is not present here on earth, I still feel his presence. I see his beautiful smile in my mind and know that he is proud of how I am raising my daughters. I have tried to cultivate an interest in sports or activities that match their abilities. I practice with them and drive them to events just like Dad did for me. Many times I hear myself repeating what he taught me to say before a race. *Take a deep breath, say a prayer, tell yourself you can do this, and then run the race (or hit the tennis ball or shoot the basket).*

Running the races of life has taught me many things. No two people will ever run the exact same race. When you are given victories, rejoice and be thankful. When you are handed defeats, accept them and try harder the next time. When you struggle or fall down, get back up and start moving forward again. And when a race leaves a scar on your knee or your heart, learn from the painful experience and don't quit.

When people ask me what I've learned from my life experiences, this is how I respond: "I've learned you must live one day at a time and look for the graces within it. It may be as simple as seeing a cardinal, getting a note from a friend, or witnessing the sweet smile of a child. Appreciate your mountain-top experiences, because they will not last forever. If the bottom falls out of your world, put one foot in front of the other, breathe, and keep going. And most important, hold on to your faith and pray. God does hear you and will give you the strength, courage, and hope to face whatever race you are asked to run."

So when anyone asks me, "So how is life treating you these days?" I smile and reply, "I'm still running the race."

978-0-595-42942-4
0-595-42942-4

Made in the USA
Lexington, KY
23 June 2014